∞

How to Find God
. . . and Discover Your True Self
in the Process

Dom Hubert van Zeller

How to Find God

. . . and Discover Your True Self in the Process

∞

A Handbook for Christians

SOPHIA INSTITUTE PRESS®
Manchester, New Hampshire

How to Find God...and Discover Your True Self in the Process: A Handbook for Christians is an abridged version of *The Inner Search*, published in 1957 by Sheed and Ward, New York. This edition by Sophia Institute Press contains minor editorial revisions and deletions to the original text, so that the book will be applicable to a wider audience.

Cover design: Coronation Media
in collaboration with Perceptions Design Studio.

On the cover: "Morning-light-illuminated church in Passo Gardena and the Dolomites" (237133489) © krcil / Shutterstock.com.

Sophia Institute Press
Box 5284, Manchester, NH 03108
1-800-888-9344

www.SophiaInstitute.com
Sophia Institute Press® is a registered trademark of Sophia Institute.

Nihil obstat: Dom A. M. Young, *Censor Cong. Angliae* O.S.B.
Imprimatur: H. K. Byrne, O.S.B., *Ab. Praes.*
March 6, 1956
Nihil obstat: Hubert Richards, S.T.L., L.S.S., *Censor Deputatus*
Imprimatur: George Lawrence Craven, *Epus Sebastopolis*
Westmonasterii, August 11, 1956

Library of Congress Cataloging-in-Publication Data
Van Zeller, Hubert, 1905-
    [Inner search]
    How to find God — and discover your true self in the process : a handbook for Christians / Hubert Van Zeller.
    p. cm.
Originally published: The inner search. New York : Sheed and Ward, 1957.
Includes bibliographical references.
    ISBN 0-918477-88-3 (pbk. : alk. paper)
1. Spiritual life — Catholic Church. I. Title.

BX2350.2.V1933 1998
248.4'82 — dc21   98-47883 CIP

∽

Contents

∞

How to Find God

. . . and Discover Your True Self
in the Process

Editor's Note: The biblical references in the following pages are based on the Douay-Rheims edition of the Old and New Testaments. Where applicable, quotations have been cross-referenced with the differing numeration in the Revised Standard Version, using the following symbol: (RSV =).

Chapter One

Seek God's face

The whole of our religious endeavor is contained in the psalmist's "Seek His face evermore."[1] The whole of our effort of faith, exercised throughout life, amounts precisely to this. But always to search for the face of the Lord is a course that the world does not value. At best, the world allows such a search a secondary place in a man's life.

The world judges it proper that men should search for the Lord *sometimes* — on Sundays, for example, or when faced with difficulties that unaided human powers cannot overcome. But to search after the face of the Lord *always* would be considered excessive by the world. Anything more than an intermittent search would be held by the world to suggest religious mania; in religion, one must avoid the extreme.

If the religious mind is to remain untouched by the view of the world, it must be forever returning to the primary truths of faith. For the Christian — not only for the contemplative, but for every Christian — the purpose of life is union with Christ. The Christian aim is to live to the fullest possible extent the life outlined in the Gospel. This is no distant ideal proposed

---

[1] Cf. Ps. 104:4 (RSV = Ps. 105:4).

only to mystics and saints; it is an undertaking projected every time an infant is baptized.

From the pages of the New Testament, then, the Christian must collect the material he will need for the search. In his reading, he will come to see the ideal man, Christ; and in his prayer and in his charity, he will come to model himself upon what he sees. Made in the image and likeness of God, a man can do nothing toward realizing the destiny proposed to him until he first knows what, and whom, he is meant to be like.

If to relive the Christ-life in the contemporary setting (which Providence has selected as being, of all possible settings, the one most likely to assist the process of sanctification) is the primary work of the Christian soul, then the first condition for such a life is the willingness to accept without qualification the principles laid down in the Gospel. Once you make reservations about the Sermon on the Mount,[2] you begin to explain away the whole teaching of Christ. Take out forgiveness or trust or prayer, and the Gospel falls to pieces.

So it follows that to become a Christian saint is nothing more than to take Christ's words at their face value and to live up to them. This is not solely to base human conduct on the Christian ethic; it is to have love as the guiding principle of interior and exterior lives. It is to experience inwardly, and to express outwardly, the law objectively realized in its infinite perfection by Christ. "God is love."[3]

In the Gospel is contained all the teaching necessary for sanctification. The Gospel reveals Christ to man, and Christ

---

[2] Matt. 5-7.
[3] 1 John 4:8, 16.

teaches love. There is no other way but this. The world is in darkness, but there is a light that can shine in the darkness, and we must look for it. The light is not easily seen because the world cannot comprehend the light.[4] The world follows false lights and so finds itself in ever blacker darkness.

But there is a true light that enlightens every man who comes into the world.[5] If we follow the light of Christ, and not the false lights of the world, which at times burn brighter and feel closer than the true light, we are given the power to be made the sons of God. For this was the Word made flesh: that man might be born, not of nature or of man, but of God.[6] This is love. This is the way and the truth and the life.[7] This is the light of Christ. But it is a hidden light.

Faith is always searching for charity and always searching for Christ, yet never finding full satisfaction in love and never knowing whether Christ is found. Faith is walking on the way, but not being sure about it; living for the truth, but having to make acts of faith about it; sharing the life, but feeling dead.

If the God of the Old Testament is the "hidden God"[8] mentioned by Isaiah, no less hidden is the God of the New Testament. But where Yahweh is the God of Justice and the Lord of Hosts, Christ is love. Perhaps one reason God is hidden in the New Testament as well as in the Old is that love, true love, hides itself so effectively. It is easier to submit to the power of

---

[4] John 1:5.

[5] John 1:9.

[6] John 1:12-13.

[7] John 14:6.

[8] Cf. Isa. 8:17, 54:8.

God than to share the love of God. To share the love of God calls for a more searching self-surrender.

So long as the soul gropes toward divine love as the fulfillment of its desire, it will not go far wrong. The soul may know little of truth, little of wisdom, but since the love it desires *is* truth and wisdom, it will find all there is to be found when it finds love. It will find happiness as well, although this will be incidental.

In finding love, the soul will have found Christ. In a sense, its search will be over; but in another sense, it will have just begun. The discovery of God is not like the discovery of a formula; it is more like the discovery of a direction. To know love is to embark upon something, not to bring something to a close. To find Christ is to start learning Christ. The sequence "ask, seek, knock"[9] is progressive.

∞

God places in every heart the desire to seek Him
Love hides its face from two classes of souls: the false lovers and the true. The false confuse appetite with love, and so fail to recognize the real thing when it comes to them; the true are kept in darkness about their love, and so add faith and hope to their search for it. The search in faith and hope for the love that seems to be always out of reach is in fact love already discovered.

Those, on the other hand, who look only for the gratification of their appetite are in exactly the opposite condition: they think that they have at last found love when in fact they

[9] Matt. 7:7; Luke 11:9.

have found only sensation. Instead of searching in faith and hope, they have searched in greed, and so have searched in darkness.

To be always looking in faith and hope for what is known to exist but evades discovery is not only of the essence of religion, but is also the motive of every generous adventure and the stuff of heroism. The search for the Christ-life is the supremely generous adventure, the one completely worthwhile heroism. But it would be a mistake to see in this the call merely to explore. Souls are not invited to experiment in divine love; they are invited to give themselves to it. Nothing so surely discovers divine love — or human love either, if it comes to that — as the readiness to sacrifice. The condition is immolation. For the Consecration in the Mass, the necessary preparation is the Offertory.

Love and sacrifice are not the same thing, but they are inseparable. To think of Christ and to think of the Cross is not the same thing, but the association is so close that the implication is immediate. Where love has been preached without sacrifice, it has led not to love but to license. Where Christ has been preached without the Cross, such preaching has led not toward Christ, but away from Him. And because the crucifix is to us Christians the symbol of our Faith, the service that we render as Christians is seen in terms of the crucifix. The love that we bring to Christ and the sacrifice that it costs us to bring it to Him are thought of together.

A price must be paid. The price of love is normally the price of faith. And this is as much the case in human love as in divine. The cost is the suffering of believing against all outward evidence that the prolonged search is in fact a progressive discovery. If the price of loving Christ is the pain of having to look for Him, the price of finding Him is the pain of having to share His loneliness in the Garden of Gethsemane.[10] Loneliness is the worst suffering, and if we can endure this in faith, we have as good as won our way to Him.

To be cut off from other human beings and their love, to be cut off from all sense of God and of His love, to be cut off from what one believes to be one's real self and to be lodged in the body of a ghost who has lost the power to love: this is loneliness. But loneliness is only one of the accompaniments of love. It is a sign, not the substance. Nor is loneliness the invariable sign: if it were, one might be able to recognize it more easily for what it signifies. What peace is to the right use of liberty, loneliness is to the service of God in prayer.

What costs the soul most is not the service itself, or the love itself, or the suffering itself, but the sense of serving badly, loving badly, or suffering badly. What God wants is not only the acts of service, love, and suffering, but the acts of resignation to personal insufficiency. For the soul to know that the whole purpose is to search for God, and at the same time to see how half-hearted its search is, must lead either to dependence or to defeat. If the soul makes use of this knowledge and trusts in God, it learns humility. If the soul makes use of the light only in order to be miserable, it exchanges the darkness of faith for the darkness of self. The grace of true humility is sacrificed for the false comfort of self-pity.

When a man sinks himself in his pain, all he is doing is trying to find pleasure. He is running away from the pain that was

---

[10] Matt. 26:36-40.

designed to be the means of his happiness. When a man accepts the humiliation that his suffering brings him, he is looking not for pleasure but for reality. Just as it is weakness to rest in one's own misery, so it is strength to make of one's own nothingness the material for confidence in God. Just as self-pity is the only kind of pity that is entirely useless, so confidence in God is the only kind of confidence that is sure proof against disappointment.

Confidence in one's power to go on indefinitely searching for God in faith is not confidence in God. Confidence in the sufferings involved in such a search is not confidence in God. Confidence in "the future" is not confidence in God. There is only one confidence in God, and that is the kind that combines faith and hope and expresses itself in works of love. If souls were allowed to feel whole-hearted in their search for God, they would begin to feel self-confident as well — self-confident not necessarily in their ability to find, but certainly in their ability to look.

There is nothing that human nature will not turn to for a sense of security, and there is satisfaction to be found even in unsatisfied striving. It is because there is so little satisfaction in this striving of faith that those who persevere in it are proved to be souls of love. If there were satisfaction in the work, what would there be to show that they were not persevering for the sake of the satisfaction? What would there be yet to look for if the mere search brought the satisfaction of discovery?

But God keeps souls fumbling and stumbling, always on the edge of discovering the object of their desire, but always painfully aware of their empty-handedness, precisely because He wants them to go on in the work for His sake, and for His sake alone. Perseverance is conditioned not by satisfaction, but by dissatisfaction. If we were satisfied that we had found what we wanted, we would stop wanting.

"Seek for the Lord while He may be found; call upon Him while He is near."[11] Yes, but in faith we must find Him; in faith we must call upon Him. The relationship between the loving soul and God is such that presence is taken for absence, light for darkness, nearness for separation, and discovery for loss. "My soul has thirsted for the strong living God," cries the psalmist. "When shall I come and appear before the face of God? My tears have been my bread day and night while it was said to me each day, 'Where is thy God?' . . . Why are you troubled, my soul? . . . Hope in God."[12] And in the same psalm, there is the suggested explanation of this troubled search: "Deep calleth upon deep. . . . With me is prayer to the God of my life. I will say to God, 'Thou art my support.' "[13]

Moses and his followers were continually within a few days' journey of the Promised Land, but for forty years they had to look for it. The Magi were in Jerusalem when Christ was only a few miles away from them at Bethlehem, but they had to look for Him. The love of God was not far from the zealous Saul of Tarsus, but before he could be Paul, he had to look for it.

"Yes," you may say, "but there was always the light from God to guide these people in their search: the Jews in the wilderness had their pillar of fire to lead them through their darkest night, the Magi had their star, and Saul was enlightened on

---

[11] Isa. 55:6.

[12] Ps. 41:3-4, 6 (RSV = Ps. 42:2-3, 5).

[13] Ps. 41:8, 9-10 (RSV = Ps. 42:7, 8-9).

the way to Damascus.[14] With us it is different: our way is hidden, and it seems just a matter of chance whether we find it or lose it." The Jews, despite all the light that they received, for the most part walked in darkness; indeed theirs was all the deeper because of their disobedience, superstitions, and lack of faith.[15] The Magi enjoyed the light of the star while they were in the desert, but when they came to the Holy City, they had no star: it was then that they had to inquire and make their acts of faith.[16] The light that brought conversion to Saul brought also blindness for a time: the light was too strong for him, so he had to find his way in darkness.[17]

We look for Christ in darkness, and in darkness He reveals Himself. We flounder in unsatisfied longing, and in our floundering we discover love. We think we have lost faith and hope, when in our seeming faithlessness and hopelessness we discover true faith and hope. Would not our eyes even get used to the face of God if they saw it all the time?

The withholding is the condition of the revelation: the blindness is the condition of the vision. Inwardly and outwardly man wrestles with his human limitations, only to learn in the end that they are the means of his liberation. Outwardly he is, as he thinks, so cramped by the circumstances of his life that he cannot render to God the service that he longs to give. Inwardly he feels so empty that his longing for outward expression diverts the energy that he feels should be directed solely

[14] Exod. 13:21; Matt. 2:1-2, 9; Acts 9:3-7.
[15] Cf. Deut. 9:13, 16.
[16] Matt. 1:2.
[17] Acts 9:8.

toward God. He is out of his element either way. He does not know which of the two unfamiliar, yet familiar, courses to follow. He is in darkness.

But all the time the outward, because it represents God's will, is leading to the soul's sanctification. All the time the inward, because it also represents God's will, is detaching the soul from itself. The two-edged sword of grace is dividing man from his misconceptions and from himself. Man, meanwhile, feels only the thrust of the sword; he feels nothing of the liberty that the action of the sword is bringing about.

To the searcher in faith, nothing is purely temporal, purely material. Every outward thing reflects the eternal, the supernatural. Nothing of the creature is insignificant when the origin of its being is seen to be God. If its end is seen to be the expression of the glory of God, everything is significant. Taken in themselves only, without relation to their meaning in God, all things might be said to be valueless. Significance and insignificance, truth and falsehood, reality and unreality: these qualities are determined solely by the relation they bear toward the being of God. Leave God out, and nothing has any meaning whatever.

Through the thicket of material cares, human activities, and secular and distracting circumstances, man must search for the light of supernatural purpose which shines in the sky behind it. Once he sees the twigs and branches lit up from the far side, he knows that the cares were material only because he made them so, that the activities were human only because he failed to see them as divine, and that the circumstances were secular and distracting only because he let in the world and failed to make use of it as a mounting block to God. In the design of God, all these things are as supernatural in purpose as the light that falls upon them.

But man is so busy looking at the objects immediately in front of him, that he misses the light that gives them their true quality. Without this light, there are no perspectives: all is seen in the dimension of the senses — flat and entirely false.

∞

You must persevere in your search for God

"Let all who seek Thee rejoice and be glad in Thee; and let such as love Thy salvation say always, 'The Lord be magnified.' "[18] We search in this life for truth, goodness, beauty, and love. When we come across these things on earth, we see a little (but only a little) of God in them. Although we know we must leave no stone unturned, no landscape unexplored, we are easily disappointed. We know that God is under the stones and in the landscape, but the temptation to substitute other things for God is too much for us. And then, when we have made the substitution, we are more disappointed than before. We find ourselves with nothing but a stone and a landscape.

If we are humble and have a grain of hope left, we begin again in our search for the real and the lovable. It is harder the second time. But for all our failure to discover what we want, we do in the end discover one thing: the only thing in life that is worth doing is searching. Experience teaches us nothing else. The man in the Gospel who went digging for his buried treasure had already found it.[19]

[18] Ps. 39:17 (RSV = Ps. 40:16).
[19] Matt. 13:44.

Chapter Two

Become your true self

There are a few moments in life when it strikes us suddenly and with great force that we are not in the least the people we had thought ourselves to be. "I have been a stranger to myself all my life," we say, "and now at last I know who I am." Then the vision fades, and we do not know who we are.

If the search after God is a drawn-out labor, the search after self is no less. Indeed, although the avenues of approach are different, the discovery of God is at the same time the discovery of self. In some cases, although more rarely, the discovery of self *leads to* the discovery of God.

The first step toward knowing who I am meant to be is to know who I am *not* meant to be. And it is this person, this false identity, whom I carry around for the greater part of my life under the mistaken conviction that this is I myself, the real me, who has to be repudiated. That is why it is so important, when the moment of self-recognition passes and the vision leaves little or no memory of the figure presented, to hang on to the knowledge that I am not what I supposed.

From the days of my childhood, when make-believe came naturally to me and there were a hundred different parts that I could play, a single, if shadowy, individual emerged from among all the possible individuals, and I decided to be that individual. *I* decided. The identification, the projection of a human being into an imaginary being, was mine. Whether in childhood, adolescence, youth, or maturity, the moment of choice came. And the chances are that I chose according to self and not according to grace. No wonder the chances are that I chose wrong.

Had I waited, had I prayed, had I looked in the mind of God for the person who bore my name, I would have been true. But instead of conforming to a reality, I have had to shape myself according to something that is without substance. It is like trying to cut out a piece of cardboard to match a wisp of smoke.

And now there is much to unlearn. To go back to the point of departure is, humanly speaking, impossible. Or rather, to go back only to find that there is nobody there; the characters I could have been have vanished. There is nobody to choose from: there is only myself upon the stage, and I do not know who I am. That make-believe which came naturally to me as a child whenever I wanted to draw upon it has for so long been with me in adult life as a settled and serious habit that I cannot see myself apart from what it shows me. I wonder if I can see anything apart from what it shows me. The faculty has changed from being a thing of pure fancy, a game, and has come to be a tyranny. It has imposed an image.

And yet, at the back of my mind, I have always suspected that this image might be false. Although I have labored to give it solidity by seeing it as the outward response to an ideal, by living it in obedience to a vocation, by professing it as an interpretation of a loyalty, I have always wondered in my heart of hearts whether a different ideal, a different vocation, or a different loyalty might not have produced a firmer and truer personification. Or perhaps the ideal, the vocation, and the loyalty have all along been the right ones, while the response, the obedience, and the interpretation have been wrongly conceived.

There must be men of genius in the world who have got no further than being men of talent. There must be souls capable of sanctity in the world who have got no further than being souls of goodness. How is it that we can be so second-rate in the lives we have chosen to lead, when in our calmest and truest moments we know that we are capable of the heights? Nearly always it is because *we* have chosen the lives we lead — or the way of leading them — and have not allowed God to do the choosing for us.

The mistake lies in refusing to look at the alternative that God offers, in case it might be an alternative that we do not want. We prefer to do our own will, even though it involves a second-rate performance, than to do the will of God, which carries with it the promise of holiness and happiness. We know only our own desire; happiness and holiness can look after themselves.

But our own immediate desire may bear little relation to our own true selves. Our true selves can become so used to bowing before the immediate desire that they grow to be unrecognizable — either to us or to anyone else. It is in this way that a man becomes estranged from himself. And because he is unknown to himself and to others, he ends up living alone in a world of shadows. There is nobody so alone as the man who, not having found God, cannot even find himself.

But there is another kind of mistaken identity, which, although arising out of conditions opposite from the ones we have been considering, produces in the individual the same unrealities. The people here considered are those who make the right choice originally, and who then spend the rest of their lives regretting it. Such souls are constantly harassed by the conviction that their lives would be more satisfactory both from their own point of view and from God's if one of the other alternatives had been followed. Such souls miss their chances for holiness and happiness, not because they are in the wrong place and know it, but because they are in the right place and will not admit it. Where the others failed in placing too much reliance upon the character that their imagination drew for them, these latter fail in placing too little reliance upon the opportunity that their choice of life has opened up to them. It amounts to the same in the end: both classes of soul, discounting the Providence of God, are aliens to their true vocation.

For a man to be a stranger in his own home, he does not have to be misunderstood by his family; it is quite enough that he should be misunderstood by himself. And how can he understand himself if he is always looking at ghosts of himself from a previous existence that never was? For a man to be second-rate in the vocation to which he is called, he does not have to be unskilled or idle; it is quite enough that his mind should be on a vocation to which he is not called. How can a man produce the best that is in him unless he knows that he can do so in the vocation that he follows?

How shall a man know who he is if he disguises his voice even when he talks to himself? How shall a man know what he is like if, every time he comes near to seeing himself, he turns his back?

How shall a man lead the life he is called to lead if he is always listening to the calls that summon other people? How shall a man follow the call of grace if he is always getting in front of grace and expecting grace to follow?

How shall a man find peace of mind if he has no mind of his own to put it in? How can he possess a mind of his own if his life is lived in a world that is not his own? How can there be any security for a man whose anchorage is in a dream?

How shall a man distinguish between a voice and an echo, between a being and an image, between inspiration and impulse, between the living word and the dead formula, between grace and delusion, or between the means and the end, unless he can say that with his whole heart he is ready to face the true and denounce the false? If he is not ready to do this, everything to him will be guesswork. And he will never know himself.

Before a man can have the wool drawn away from his eyes, he must admit to himself and to God that the wool is there — and that, in all probability, he put it there. But this is just what most of us shrink from admitting. We pretend that we can see, and therefore our blindness is all the greater.

If we truly saw nothing at all of ourselves and of God's purpose for us, we would not be so bad off; at least we would not pretend: we would have to submit to being shaped and led by God. The trouble is that we see a little, and see it wrong. What we see is mysterious enough to appeal, but not transparent enough to be seen through. Anyway, it acts as an effective alternative to being shaped and led by God.

How to Find God

We do not rebel openly against being shaped and led by God. We do not say, "I see God's way, and it is not for me." We say instead, "I do not see God's way clearly, so I am justified in following what I do see of my own." The little that we see of our own way is seen in the mirror of self, and seen therefore in reverse.

If a man of the world can play the man of God, if the monk can play the arbiter of fashion, if the libertine can play the martyr, then there seems to be no end to the possible transpositions. Whom do we all want to deceive? It is not God — so presumably it is other people and ourselves. Buy why? What is the point of a life that has no reality except in the impression — and a false one — that is registered in the brain of another person? And what is the point of deceiving ourselves with a being whose existence has come out of our imagination?

A thing has reality only because it exists in the mind of God. Apart from what we are in God, we are nothing. The difference between being and nonbeing is the difference between having a place or being placeless in God. So unless I discover what I am to God, I am hidden from myself and from other people. Until I play my part as God means it to be played, I am improvising as I go along; I am performing the actions of someone who is not in the cast. I have no right to be there at all.

It would seem (to continue the simile from the theater) that the man who stands the best chance of being true to his nature is in fact the professional actor. He plays different parts, knowing that each one is a part, and has no intention of deceiving either God, his audience, or himself. But not everybody is called to be a professional actor. And even for the actor there is the problem of discovering, in addition to discovering the parts that suit him best, the person he is meant to be. It is not our professional lives that qualify, nor our private lives, but our whole lives.

Life is not a question of playing the hero one night, the jester the next night, and some sort of self-devised part in between. There is a relentless unity about life that forbids this. So if we are the same person throughout the week, what if we are the wrong person — not the person God wants to see when He thinks of us (as He constantly does, or we would not exist at all)?

Our tragedy is that although we detect a false note in our Hamlet, we have to go on playing Hamlet. It is too late to start playing Falstaff.[20] For most of us, there is nothing to do but play the same part we have always played, but to play it differently. Life has caught us, and there is no escape. At least let us not escape again into unreality.

Life does not demand much more of us than constancy and truth. If we remain fixed in our determination to follow the truth where we see it, we can hardly go far wrong. It is the people whose principles are dictated by mood, and whose view of truth is therefore prejudiced, who make failures of their lives.

Uncertain though our true function in life may be, the stage is largely set for us. In the last analysis, our success lies not in the quality of our performance, but in our sincerity as performers. What God wants of us is not that we should win our way to the top of the bill, but that we should be true to the

[20] Hamlet and Falstaff are, respectively, characters in William Shakespeare's *Hamlet* and *Henry IV*.

role in which He has cast us. Although our names be in the smallest print, we can yet be true.

What God wants is not the career that has helped to develop the character, but the character that has helped to develop the career. I am a person before I am a profession. I must be true to myself as a man before I can be true to myself as a monk. I must be true to myself as *this* man before I can be true to anything at all.

It comes, then, to this: although we may have muddled our way into the wrong company and have been playing the wrong part, we still have the chance of giving a true presentation of the right life as God sees it. Life for most of us means that we have to go on and on playing out our part against scenery that is no longer of our own choice and which we feel to be entirely inappropriate. It means playing to an audience that has not necessarily the least interest in us, but has been forced by circumstances to be present while we perform. It means we will have no idea how the plot is going to work out, and that we know only the lines of the speech that we happen to be reciting. Even the costume and the makeup are not of our own choosing. We have nothing to bring to the stage but ourselves. So it must be *our* selves and not other people's. Nobody can be my understudy, and I can be nobody else's.

∞

Finding your true self means conforming to God's will

Whether I know myself or not, whether I like my life or not, I and my life will be judged on the single issue of conformity. Am I one with God's will? Have I conformed to the pattern of God's love?

For me to point to a substitute self of my own devising and to say, "But he gives a better performance than anything I could have managed" or, "I thought people would prefer him" or, "I never liked the idea of what in fact was given me to do" will be no excuse. The parable of the talents[21] is the reply to such evasions.

One thing above all I must not say, for it would be more untrue than any of the above objections, is: "I feel happier in the part I have made for myself." This, although it may have been the reason for my self-deception and the grounds of my expectation, is a manifest lie. I am never happier when I am not myself. I can be happy only when I have found myself, never when I am lost, and seldom when I am in doubt. Wanting what God wants is the only true peace, the only happiness worth having. If I want to be someone whom God has not thought of as me, I am heading away from happiness and peace. I am heading away from my true self.

In order for truth in the sense here discussed to become operative — that is, for the right relation between a man's inward conformity and his outward life — the inspiration, as suggested above, has to be love.

The conformity that stops short of loving conformity, and conformity to love, is a truth without life. The multiplication table is true, but it brings us no closer to God. The printed list in a railway guide may conform to the schedules of trains, but it makes no contribution to our love. If a man's appreciation of truth does not lead to charity, there is no particular point in his having it.

[21] Matt. 25:14-30.

Since love and truth are equally part of humanity, a man must, if he is to know himself truly, know himself as a man of love. My truth as a human being is commensurate with my truth as a loving human being. If I am to know myself, I must know what part love is meant to play in my life. The idea of truth leads naturally to the idea of integrity. But there can be no real integrity, which is completeness, without love. I may know a good deal about myself, I may have true principles of self-criticism, but if I know myself without knowing how to love, I know only a skeleton: the bones are mine, and they give accurate information as far as they go; the only thing left out is the person.

Thus in order that I may be my whole self, I must come to a right understanding both of my place in charity and of the place of charity in me. I must try to see how God loves His creatures and how His creatures are lovable on that account. In order, again, that I may be my true self, not only must I learn to see human and divine love in unity, but I must also express human and divine love in practice. For the complete Christian — that is, for the saint — the truth of his vocation in Christ is proved by his development in charity. For the complete Christian, service of God is no more and no less than true love. Sanctity is measured by nothing less than love — the love of Christ reproduced in the follower of Christ.

Whereas the charity of the ordinary person is a synthetic charity composed of duties, devotions, and acts of obedience and of supererogation,[22] the charity of the saint is a synthesis of

---

[22] Acts of supererogation are good works that help to develop one's spiritual and moral life, but are not morally required.

love. When we have found this integration, we have found ourselves. A man loses himself in bitterness, in alienation, in uncharity, and in disintegration; he finds himself in charity and unity.

If I feel at variance with my life, my fellowmen, my vocation, or my very self, I must rediscover my true nature, not by changing the changeable contingencies, but, rather, by trying to deepen the deeper qualities of my soul. I must draw into a single desire — the desire for God, who is love and truth — all of what I conceive to be my essential self. Love itself, truth itself, will do the rest, forming in my soul the pattern of His will. And then at last, at one within myself, I shall be able to claim that I have found my own soul.

Chapter Three

Seek lasting happiness

Although we are always being told that happiness does not consist in getting what we want in life, we are seldom told that it may well consist in wanting what we have. If it is true that what comes to us in the ordinary run of life is God's will, we have every right to find happiness in wanting to enjoy what in fact we have been given.

If the saint is the man who makes God's will his whole happiness, he can be very happy in a world where he gets God's will the whole day long. On the same principle, a man who is not a saint can be very unhappy in a world that, although providing the means for happiness, is seen apart from God and is therefore enjoyed wrongly. Whereas the saint, making God the sum of his desire, finds a relative pleasure in created good, the man of the world, making created good the sum of his desire, dooms himself to disappointment. If a man does not want more than he can get on earth, he will never be satisfied with what he can get on earth. The man who *does* want more than he can get on earth — and who wants it to the exclusion of all other claims — is easily satisfied with what he finds on earth.

Thus, to look for happiness in any direction that has an end in this life is to look, ultimately, at a blank wall. The moment we grasp this truth, we cast about for something that will do as a substitute for complete happiness in this life; we want to know if there is a second best that can be pressed to its utmost limit. It is tiresome to be told where *not* to look for happiness; is there nothing we can look *at* instead?

To turn away from the wrong sources of happiness is not the same as to turn toward the right, and to allow ourselves to stare vacantly into space is to ask for further delusion. The eye begins to focus on what it wants in some mirage world on the distant horizon, when it should be trained to look squarely at what lies immediately at hand.

This does not mean that we may not hope for the good things that are not ours but to which we have a right if we take the trouble to work for them — or we would have to rule out sanctity itself — but it does mean that we may not rest in an unreal world of our own imagination. Actuality is more productive of happiness than the ability to dream. Dreams are good enough, so long as they are ideals and not escapes. Dreams are only unfulfilled desires, and the test of their quality lies in the effect they have upon the practical side of life. Do they lead to meeting life or evading it?

The secret lies in accepting life for what it is: natural life as designed by God to be natural, supernatural as designed by God to be divine. We render to Caesar the things that are Caesar's, to God the things that are God's.[23] Creatures are to be taken *as* creatures — ordained to be creatures by God. It is only when this is rightly understood that the created order is seen to be the divine.

[23] Matt. 22:21; Mark 12:17; Luke 20:25.

"*C'est le don de voir toutes choses telles qu'elles sont,*"[24] is De Polignac's cynical definition of pessimism. But the definition can be applied too, and quite without cynicism, to the realistic approach of the Christian saint. The realist is neither optimistic nor pessimistic: he is the observer who sees in due perspective. He knows that the actual has its limitations, that the ultimate is the only thing that matters, and that the ultimate is infinite — is God.

This does not mean that in a world that is full of sorrows, we have to make the best of it by plucking chestnuts out of the fire, finding what happiness we can by getting used to the burnt taste of what we have been able to rescue. It means, rather, that we must get used to the fire and find our happiness in its warmth.

So long as our desires are not guided by enlightened reason, we are blocked; the appetite is always more compelling than satisfaction is satisfying. It is only reason, which patiently explains to the will that there are other and more lasting satisfactions waiting for it in the next life, that can ensure any sort of true happiness. Gautama Buddha[25] saw that the only means of happiness lay in the control of desire. The Greek philosophers saw this equally clearly. So also did the Christian saints. But whereas the Indian sought to eliminate desires and where the Greek sought to balance them, the Christian aims at directing his desires toward God. In practice, neither the Buddhist mystic nor the Greek philosopher can be wholly successful: the

[24] "It is the gift of seeing all things as they are."

[25] Gautama Buddha (c. 563-c. 483 B.C.), religious teacher and philosopher who lived in India and founded Buddhism.

one must always find half-stifled desires reasserting themselves and spoiling the pattern of his studied calm; the other must always be tied to an arbitrary standard of measurement and so will never be sure that his balance of desires (which, in any case, are liable to change) is the right one. It is only the Christian who can know what to want, and where to find it. Nor, for this search, does the Christian have to be either a mystic or a philosopher. All he has to be is a Christian.

∞

Fear can be an obstacle to the search for happiness

Allowing that happiness is not in the abundance of things to be possessed, not in meat and drink, not in anything that rust and moth can get at,[26] what now? Allowing that a soul awakens to the truth about the kingdom of God being within,[27] about the peace of Christ being the only true peace,[28] about being content with one's pay and not being envious,[29] how is the soul to proceed that has found this true philosophy, this new happiness?

The discovery of happiness, like the discovery of sorrow, is meant to unite a soul more closely with God and with other people. When it fails to do this, it fails itself: it has, as has suffering, the reverse effect of what it was designed to promote. If it does not make men generous, a taste of either happiness or sorrow makes men selfish. The large-hearted expand; the

---

[26] Cf. Matt. 6:20.

[27] Luke 17:21.

[28] Cf. Eph. 2:14.

[29] Luke 3:14.

mean contract. When happiness is misunderstood to the extent of being hoarded and wallowed in, it ultimately peters out. When unhappiness is hoarded and wallowed in, it ultimately becomes the worst sort of unhappiness, which is lonely self-will. Happiness and unhappiness, clumsily handled, can be very misleading.

There are those who, waking up suddenly to a new happiness and to a hitherto unknown view of the meaning of life, feel ill at ease. People who have been more or less happy all their lives may not understand how this can be so, but it is nevertheless the case, and the contingency must be allowed for. Whereas congenitally happy people feel that they have been born during a summer holiday and that it has remained a summer holiday ever since, those who are new to happiness feel they have taken an excursion ticket to the sea and have missed the train back.

It is not those who take their good fortune for granted that we are considering at the moment; our immediate concern is with those who question their claim to happiness, and who consequently feel themselves to be strangers wherever they are. It is not that they mind having missed their train back — indeed they would not go over the past again for anything — but that they are so conditioned by their experience of life as to be virtually incapable of making use of the happiness that is theirs. Unless such souls are ready to forget their previous experience and to leave themselves in the hands of God, they will turn the present into the past and repeat their former mistakes. They will be back in their old misery with the added misery of having missed their chance. In order to meet the new order, the old order has to be reversed. If wartime controls that served in the emergency are resorted to in times of peace, the result is not peace but war; the conflict is now inward instead of outward. Souls who are uneasy in peace create for themselves their private wars: they dare not trust the terms of the treaty, they are suspicious of disarmament, and they fear a return to hostility. It means that they are happier in unhappiness, more secure in the atmosphere that is familiar to them.

If knowledge brings with it at first a sense of loss, so also does happiness. When we have reached a certain stage in our experience of happiness, it is as though what we had thought to be a statue in the distance has in fact turned out to be a person. Although the person may be someone we love, we know that we can never again enjoy the illusion about the statue. We may try to put ourselves back in mind to what we were before, but all we get out of this is to lose the happiness we might have had. Nor can we still look forward to something we have already rejected.

At the root of all this is fear: we are afraid to shed what we have known in return for a new responsibility toward something that is unknown. There is a homesickness in happiness, a loneliness that can well destroy the capacity for joy. So much opportunity — too much at once — is opened up, and the soul shrinks from its liberty.

Only when a man has fully grown into his happiness, and when it has become to him a protective covering, has he nothing more to fear. By this time, he knows that his happiness comes from God and that he must take it with him to God again. If perfect love casts out fear,[30] so in the end does true

---

[30] 1 John 4:18.

happiness. But in neither case is fear expelled automatically. If his love and his happiness are to grow within him, a man must resolutely turn his back on fear.

∞

The soul enjoys a higher degree of happiness than the body

Another factor to be considered in relation to human happiness is the unequal distribution of man's powers of enjoyment. The rational part of man has the advantage over the sensitive part: the spirit can share the pleasures of the senses in a way in which the senses are not able to share the pleasures of the spirit. And since it is not often that Cordelia gets the better of Goneril and Regan,[31] the proposition is worth a moment's examination.

Take the pleasure of study, for example, as compared with the pleasure of taking drugs. In the first case, the physical faculties enjoy next to nothing of the mind's satisfaction: the pleasure of speculation, argument, knowledge, and so on belong to the intellectual order alone. In the second case, the mind is able to appreciate the body's comfort as well as its own.

The body never rises above sense, and so cannot see what is going on, for good or for evil, in the soul. True, the spirit can so far debase itself as to allow the flesh to get the upper hand, and where this happens there is the inversion we call sin. Sin destroys the soul; the senses, by themselves, can destroy only the tissues that make up the brain. But of course it can come to the same in the end.

[31] Characters in William Shakespeare's *King Lear*.

So if it is true that beyond a certain point of satisfaction, the physical is found to anaesthetize the moral side of man's nature, it will be necessary to find a harmony of appetites that will preserve due order — which will ensure the right relation among reason, will, emotion, and instinct, and so dispose for true happiness.

The purpose of spirituality is not to exclude the body from happiness, but to get it to share happiness and elevate it. The body will never enjoy the transports that are experienced by the soul, but at least it can catch some of the overflow. St. John of the Cross,[32] discussing states of prayer, accounts for the sweetness experienced in the senses by pointing to the more elevated exercise that goes on in the superior faculties of the soul.

Not until the resurrection of the body will man be fully explained, fully complete. Then will the senses come into their own; then will they find their place in the happiness of the soul. But even while the body is united to the spirit in this life, there is a harmony to be achieved that makes for human happiness, and it is our duty to find it.

For the will to frustrate the body beyond a certain point is to make not for harmony but for rebellion. The senses may, for a time, be subdued by mortification, but the danger is that they will wait their opportunity and, on a day when they are not mortified, will lash back. And the claim that the senses then make will be not for higher satisfactions but for lower. The power of being able to contribute to the satisfactions of

---

[32] St. John of the Cross (1542-1591), mystical Doctor and joint founder of the Discalced Carmelites.

the spirit is at the same time a power to destroy the satisfactions of the spirit. The senses can wreck the happiness of man. Indeed, it is nearly always because of the demands of the senses that the chances of happiness are forfeited.

Not only are the senses very often the enemy of the spirit, but they are often their own enemy as well: sin harms the whole man, body as well as soul. Sin, if only people realized it at the time of temptation, is as much the enemy of natural happiness as it is the enemy of supernatural happiness. All along the line, even in this world, man is worse off for every sin that he commits.

While perfect happiness is a state reserved for the next world, there is a perfect human happiness that arises out of the exercise of faith, hope, and charity. It is not the end of our faith, hope, and charity — the end of these virtues is God — but it may well be looked forward to as a consequence. To make a cult of human happiness would be folly; to accept it with gratitude as a byproduct of the service of God is wisdom. To deny oneself the chances of finding true human happiness would be folly; to accept the limitations of one's happiness under human conditions is wisdom.

To sacrifice one kind of happiness in order to attain to another is part of life itself and the experience of every man; to sacrifice one's own happiness for the sake of another person's is heroic charity. To sacrifice it for the love of God is sanctity. It is one of the paradoxes of human experience that those who have handed over their happiness to God, and who are prepared to be unhappy for the rest of their lives as victims bearing witness to His love, are in fact the happiest of all. So it would seem that to make God the whole of one's desire, to exhaust every appetite in His love, is the one way of realizing the happiness that God has planned for the human heart.

Free from the alloy of self-interest and the undeclared flaws of mental reservation, the metal of the soul is now entirely at the disposal of God. It is only when this stage has been reached that material can be plunged into the heat, melted down, and recast in the mold that is waiting for it. It is only now that this iron of our fallen natures will be unresisting. And it is only now that we shall find ourselves in our true happiness.

The faculty of reason, thus transformed, sees now in a new fashion. The faculty of will, purified of false hungers, stretches out with a new intensity. The emotional faculties, settled at last in their true function, are now no longer an obstacle but a help. And the senses, drawn toward a beauty that before was obscured by concupiscence, find satisfaction only in the good of creation, recoiling instinctively from what has been turned by man's malice into bad.

That element of impermanence that right through his life has prevented happiness from being the complete state that he conceives it to be, is, with the grace of transforming union, no longer a shadow to his joy. United to the will of God, which is his own will now and his own happiness, he anticipates the joy of Heaven and has no further worries about the instability of human affairs. Now does that eternal love, which all along has been his inspiration and by which he lives and moves and has his being,[33] show itself in its own light. Still will this revelation of love be beyond understanding, still intermittently apprehended, still for the most part blinding to the mind and

[33] Acts 17:28.

causing darkness rather than light; yet will it convey to the soul, obscurely but most forcibly, the nothingness of creatures and the everything of God.

By the light of this grace, the soul comes to see not only that the search for happiness which has engaged every energy has in fact been the search for nothing other than God, but also, and more significantly, that it has been God Himself who, working secretly within the soul, has done the seeking. When God is known to be at once the Seeker and the Sought — and so when God is seen to be the *All* — then can the soul be freed from self and find its happiness in the happiness of God.

Chapter Four

❧

Learn to see God all around you

By looking too closely at a thing, you can come to see it wrongly. Or rather, you miss its size and quality in relation to everything else. You have to be at the right distance from a mountain, just as you have to be at the right distance from a molehill, if you are to see it for what it is. If you bury your face in either a mountain or a molehill, you may come to know a lot about the soil, but you add little to your knowledge of the thing itself.

Man is so close to creation that he tends to miss the point of it. In order to see the significance of the material world, you have to stand back and look at it in terms of the spiritual world. Unless you see the universe in its setting — unless you are constantly aware of its origin and end — you see it only as a biological fact.

Creation is the echo of God's word, a part of the revelation of Himself, a work of divine art, an idea in the mind of God made actual. Man is blind if he sees all this merely as a physical phenomenon, bound by the law of time. Heaven and earth will pass away, but God's word will not pass away.[34] The temporal

---

[34] Matt. 24:35; Mark 13:31.

must be understood in relation to the eternal, or it is not un-derstood at all.

No less blind is the man who, denying the reality of created beauty, spurns the world as not worth looking at. He may want the spiritual life before all else, he may spend every available hour in prayer, but he has to live on this earth for a time. The sooner he cultivates a bifocal vision, the better. He cannot live by throwing himself over the horizon.

To look without prejudice upon the world around you calls for a more than human judgment. If you are not to confuse the essential with the accidental, the portrait with the caricature, the absolute with the relative, the mountain with the mole-hill, you will need the light of grace. You need supernatural in-sight in order to understand the natural. It is hard enough for the Christian, with the help of grace, to see what creation is all about, but for the hedonist and the humanist, it must be almost impossible. To the man unenlightened by grace, the outward is so shiningly clear, so solid and defined, so unmistakable. No wonder he takes it to be the whole story.

Even the man of prayer can get swept off his feet by the false substance of created things. "This is real, and everything else is nonsense," he can hear himself say as he is caught up by a singer into the magic of a song or as he responds to the pas-sion of great acting. "Nothing of the past or future matters — neither human misery nor obedience nor self-control nor ac-cepted convention. This alone is worth living for; this is expe-rience at last."

Practical judgment, backed by the evidence of previous failure, may help to prevent the overstressing of one thing and the understressing of another. But it is only by supernatural standards that the contingencies of human life can be assessed. And even then there are misconceptions. The light of grace does not claim to expose every inconsistency. But when it does, it makes us acutely uncomfortable living with it.

As the result of Original Sin, there is nothing that we can approach and say, "I am dispassionate about this; I have a completely open mind." The mind of fallen man is never entirely open, and the more a man sins, the narrower his mind becomes. The more a man sins, the less dispassionate he is.

Always, and perhaps so deeply lodged below the surface of our natures that we are genuinely unconscious of its operation, there is the tendency not only to preview and prejudge what is coming toward us, but also to notice only the exaggerations in what we see and to base our judgment upon them (which is more unfortunate, since it may not be so readily corrected).

When our Lord speaks about the eye being the lamp of the body, and the eye being sound,[35] He means for us to use the light to see the whole rather than the part, the normal rather than the exceptional, the real rather than the superficial. But for this, the eye must be enlightened by grace and prayer. Eyes are not sound from birth. It is so much easier to focus attention on the features that shine, that stand out, or that look odd. The question is, are these the essential features, or are they merely accidental? The immediately visible is seldom the main issue, and although the outward exaggeration may often be an indication of the inward reality, it may also be a screen put up to hide what is its exact opposite.

[35] Matt. 6:22; Luke 11:34.

For example, it is commonplace that the sad man will often show to the world over-boisterous high spirits, the weak man a mulish obstinacy, and the romantic man a studied indifference. Not only do these people reveal to the outside world qualities and dispositions that run contrary to their true natures, but they also put up these facades to deceive themselves. This has something to do with the law of compensation.

The compensation is frequently so secret and occult that those practicing it are as much in the dark as those who judge by its results. The sound eye, consequently, must be trained to look at creation, at others, and at self in the light of grace and faith. Without this light, we are all too prone to see what we want to see and no more — which means that we are sitting in the dark.

In every area of life that requires decisions — but particularly in that area of life that relates to spiritual decisions — there must be distinctions; the mind must exercise its critical faculty and distinguish between what should be followed and what rejected. Decision is nothing other than this. But we incline toward making the wrong distinctions; we take the superficial because it is nearer, or more obvious, or the one that will give less trouble. And so we go on to make the wrong decision. It is important that we should see what we are distinguishing, and why.

When we are faced with created effects that we are expected to handle, expected to marshal into some sort of pattern, it is important that we should see them in the light of their primary cause and final end. Otherwise we shall not be bearing witness to creation, but hindering its plan. And *created effects* means people, situations, policies, crises — anything that arises from or contributes to the inward and outward complexity that we call life.

How can I help another if I take him to be what his affectations tell me he is? How can I be a fruitful member of the unit to which I belong if I judge it only by its weaknesses and not by its strength? How can I give sound and objective advice on projects that I consider in the light of self-interest? How, in other words, can I give glory to God in His creation if I insist upon seeing it in terms of myself instead of in terms of the planning mind that orders it?

The upshot of all this is that I must get into the habit of measuring by the standard of God's will all that is presented to me, not only by the life of the senses, but also by the life of the intellect. So far as the senses go, the process is fairly straightforward: I can usually tell whether I am responding to created beauty because I am physically attracted or because I am stirred to worship God. The gap between greed and wonder is fairly wide. The difficulty comes when the perceptions are not physical but intellectual.

Self operates brazenly in the senses; it operates more subtly, but no less powerfully, in the intellect. If I have reason to suspect the apparently legitimate claims of the body, I have all the more reason to suspect the assumptions of the mind — those that are not immediately confirmed by Revelation anyway.

This means that I must hold up many generally accepted slogans to the light of grace. I must be ready to think a subject through to its conclusion, taking nothing for granted on the way. I must beware of the slick and oversimplified on the one hand and of the speculative and overelaborate on the other.

Now, there is nothing more boring than having to sift and probe and question. Instinctively we shrink from the man who makes a process of everything. Few subjects can stand up to minute analysis. By the time we have taken an idea to bits and reassembled it, we have lost interest in it; we do not greatly care whether it is true or false. But, alas, it is what we as Christians have to do nevertheless: look into things — not merely look *at* them — and maintain in faith the interest that in nature tends to flag.

And such a course need not be as dull as it looks on paper. We are not expected to make a study of every political movement or to doubt the sincerity of the secular authority under which we live. What the sound eye must do is to look squarely at the world's headlines and see whether they conform to the Sermon on the Mount. What the sound eye has to do is look closely at anything that suggests the partisan, at anything that savors of propaganda. Every heresy in history has been launched precisely because Christian souls have failed to make the right distinctions. Every humanist ideology has its root in a wrong way of looking at created good. Every malpractice among Christian people springs from an unwillingness to take the creature for what it is and the Creator at His word.

∞

Created things point to God

Just as, when standing before a brick wall, you can think of the cement as either holding the bricks together or keeping them apart; just as, when standing before a staircase, you can think of the steps as carrying people upward or bringing them down; just as, when looking at the sky at night, you can think of it as darkness pierced by points of light or as stars shining against a background of darkness, so creation to you will depend upon how you look at it. See it as placed there for your satisfaction, and satisfaction eludes you. See it as a clue to be followed up and as the most elemental pointer to the nature of God; see it as a harmony with which you can combine by bringing your own personal note of praise; see it as a mystery that has its whole and sole explanation in love, and you pay God the twofold homage of using for its proper purpose what He has made and of finding your satisfaction in Him instead of in yourself.

In order that good things may not be wrongly apprehended and that bad things may not be seen as good, nature itself sometimes has to take second place to a more direct system of revelation. It is as though the very rhythm of nature, designed to lead man's mind to the mind of the Creator, sometimes has the reverse effect of what was intended; it is as though man's mind were hypnotized by the regular swing of the pendulum, as though he is lulled to sleep by the even throb. And so you get miracles.

Every now and then, God suspends the physical laws of His universe and brings man's mind up short against the manifestly spiritual. This is to teach man not to be a fool, not to be more of a materialist than he can help, not to take the natural order as possessing the complete answer to the problem of being. Faced with the miraculous, man is given more than a mere hint, more than just another opportunity of stirring up his devotional life, more than the immediate good that the specific miracle conveys. He is being invited — compelled even — to say, "Here is a law in operation that is more powerful than the one I know from my experience. I must bow to it." He is being compelled to say, "Whatever I have learned from observing the world about me is as nothing compared with the knowledge that must be stored up in the world to which this phenomenon bears witness." He is being invited (not compelled this time) to say, "I do not understand, but one day I shall understand; and in the meantime I believe and love and ask for nothing more."

The bush goes on burning, so that Moses, seeing it unconsumed, may make his act of faith in the underlying purpose of God and may bring his tribute of love.[36] The fleece remains dry when by the rules of nature it should be wet, and remains wet when by the rules of nature it should be dry, so that Gideon may see not the fleece in front of him, but the principle that rules the rules of nature, and may bring his tribute of service and love.[37] The servant of Elisha is granted to see through the visible sky to the army of angels hidden behind the sky. And so on right down through the history of man until you come to the miracle of Fatima.[38] And so it will go on to the end.

"Lord, that I may see" — and he sees.[39] But does seeing always lead to love? Man has a way of evading the lesson of

---

[36] Exod. 3:2-4.

[37] Judg. 6:37-40.

[38] Fatima, Portugal, is the site of several apparitions of the Blessed Virgin Mary to three children, beginning in May 1917. During one of the apparitions, hundreds of onlookers saw the sun begin to spin and turn various colors and then rush toward the earth momentarily before returning to its place in the sky.

[39] Mark 10:51-52.

revelation. The climax to which the whole thing is meant to point is nearly always missed: love remains unlearned. From the laws of nature and from the instances in which the laws of nature are transcended and suspended, man sometimes gets as far as learning about the folly of trusting in earthly securities. But he seldom learns about trusting wholly in the divine.

Man sees the wonder of creation all around him and gets used to it. But he can get just as used to the wonder of the miraculous. The attitudes of mind go together; they are indeed the same attitude. The worldliness that takes the natural for granted takes also the supernatural for granted. The Israelites who looked no further than their leeks and melons while in Egypt were the same who looked no further than their miraculous helpings of manna when they were in the wilderness.[40] There is this fatal quality in man: he rests content in what his senses tell him of security.

But the outward is given to us so that we may find our way to the inward; the temporal, so that we may acknowledge the eternal. "The visible things of God's creation are clearly seen," not so that we may feast our eyes on what is beheld, but so that our minds may mount to the thought of what is invisible. "For the things that are seen are temporal, but the things that are not seen are eternal."[41]

The danger to which a materialistic age is liable is not only the obvious one of sacrificing spiritual demands to the demands of the body. More significant, it is the danger that such a want of balance between body and soul will result in the

[40] Num. 11:5-6.
[41] 2 Cor. 4:18.

scales' ceasing to measure. From answering to only one category of appetites, the soul will no longer be in a position to appreciate the demands of the other — let alone will it have the strength to defend and pursue them. It is then that man is "given up to a reprobate sense": he has mistaken creation and the nature of his own being.

Equally evident is the danger, in a machine age, of paying too much homage to technical skill and tangible results. Experience shows how we can come more and more to rely upon the device that saves labor, and less and less upon labor itself. And this has a blunting effect upon our assessment of values. Spiritual men constantly have to warn mankind against forgetting the Creator and worshiping the inventor. Where respect is virtually transferred from the craft to the machine that replaces the craft, you cannot help but get parallel substitutions, some of which are patently opposed to the order established for man by God. But there can be a good deal of cant about this, too.

There is nothing in itself unholy about a machine any more than there is something in itself holy about the soil. To see creation rightly, we must look at the whole of creation, not merely at the parts that are recognizable from the book of Genesis.

It is just as unbalanced to pay excessive respect to one aspect of God's material creation as it is to another. To do so is to commit idolatry. Equally unbalanced is to pay excessive disrespect to one aspect as it is to another. This is contempt. (We are here considering respect and disrespect insofar as either is *excessive* — not insofar as respect or disrespect may be merited in its degree.) While it is clearly easier to discern the finger of God in the fruit of the earth than in the product of the factory, it is nevertheless true that neither the one nor the other could have come into being independently of God.

God made the brain of man and trained it by the power of His Spirit, just as He made the soil of the field and developed it in due season. The Providence of God places one seed in the hand of the husbandman and another in the head of the engineer. Each seed that is planted by God is designed to meet a particular requirement of the human race — now a physical requirement, now a social requirement, now an economic requirement, now a cultural or educational or recreational requirement. What in effect the human race, with its gift of free will, decides to do with what comes to harvest from the planted seed is another matter.

So the empirical faculty possessed by the rational animal is to be seen as the gift of God like any other. The individual possessing it may use it or abuse it like any other gift. We, noting its operation from outside and affected to a greater or lesser degree by its achievement, may respect or despise it. One thing neither he nor we may do is ignore it. But although we may peer into the mystery of creation, it must remain to us largely a mystery. Although from Scripture we may hack out an approach to it, the avenue soon seems to become covered with growth again. "Hardly do we guess aright at the things that are upon the earth," says the book of Wisdom, "and with labor do we find the things that are before us."[42] But at least there is the suggestion that if we labor long enough, we shall get them right.

We shall never entirely mistake the world about us if we abide by the principles enunciated above: on the one hand,

[42] Wisd. 9:16.

careful to avoid being ruled by the law of the senses, and on the other, to see through the pantheistic error of taking the natural order to be an emanation of God Himself.

But the trouble for most of us comes not so much in steering clear of the extremes of misconception as rather in muddling along among marginal mistakes. It is not so much a question of sins to be confessed as of false qualities that we unthinkingly attribute every day and that come to weaken our apprehension of essential truth.

The solution to the so-called riddle of the universe is neither a scientific nor a psychological one. Basically it is a mystical one. To the materialist, a primrose is a flower and nothing more; to the mystic, it is so much more that it is barely a flower. Creation proclaims itself in such dazzling terms to the mystic that he has to look twice before he can see the creature as it presents itself to his senses.

Neither is the primrose a symbol and nothing more. Apart from its importance as evoking associations buried in the unconscious, apart from what it stands for in the psychiatrist's dictionary, it has a significance of its own. The mystic, for all his apparently fanciful flights, will appreciate this at once.

But the thing goes deeper than this. To the mystic — and in our degree, we must all be mystics if we want to see truth — the lesson that is learned from creatures, the whole meaning that creation holds for us, the point of confluence to which the created order tends, is love. Leaving out love, there would be no reason for the existence of an external world, no need for a revelation, no sense in anything, and no purpose in life. Apart from love, there would be no hope.

Chapter Five

∞

Look for God in others

If it is difficult to appreciate the inwardness of inanimate and animal nature, it is no easier to get behind the surface when it comes to dealing with rational nature. Lower creation is subtle enough, but man, the lord and finished specimen of creation, calls for quite as powerful an act of faith. Human beings, we fellow lords, must probe deep into the problems of one another's personalities. If we are to see the truth and live in charity, we shall need more than unaided human reason can supply.

On an earlier page, we considered how prone a man is to project to the world a self that he is not, in order to protect the self that he does not want to see. This tendency will make it difficult for another to penetrate to an identity whose existence is not admitted by the person whose identity it is. And when both are playing the same game, the area of error, untruth, and deception is proportionately enlarged.

Yet if the mutual exchange that rational creation demands is to be effective, a degree of interknowledge among human beings is essential. How do we come by it? Not by looking up each other's files. No one person will understand another if he regards that other as being sealed off from him by either class, nationality, age, or outlook. To posit hypothetical barriers in others is to erect an actual one in oneself. To suppose barriers within oneself is to build them up in the minds of other people.

Nor will there be any real communication if the ground of exchange is restricted to the unreal. In the dealings between man and man, there is not only much that is congenitally and unconsciously unreal, but much also that is deliberately and acceptedly unreal.

In order to see into the nature of another, it may be necessary to jettison social conventions: politeness can be the enemy of understanding. If courtesy is not the expression of charity, it may well be the disguise of uncharity. Just as awkward behavior springs either from thoughtlessness or overanxiety to please, so correct behavior springs either from interest in others or interest in self.

On the positive side, there is only one rule for the discovery of one's fellowmen, and this is an absolute and not a conditional rule. It is that one must be ready to love them.

The moment this rule is applied, the searcher is lifted out of his inhibitions, prejudices, and false apprehensions, and is prepared to accept the other person for what he is — not for what he may be, but for what he is, for what God made him. The seeker may not know what he will find, what he is letting himself in for, what he may afterward regret; but he is moving in the right direction. He is moving in the right direction because he is learning about human nature as well as about this particular representative of human nature. And he is learning also about himself and about charity. He need not worry: he will not have so much to regret.

And what of the one who is sought? He, too, the moment the rule has been applied, is laid open not only to being understood by another, but also to being understood by himself.

Charity is not like two different webs being spun by two different spiders until the webs and spiders meet; it is more like one web spun by both spiders whether the spiders happen to meet or not.

Or, to change the metaphor, mutual charity is not two mirrors facing different ways; it is one mirror reflecting different objects but facing the same way. The mirror is intended primarily for reflecting the light of God, but it also reveals the features of the people who are looking into it. Mirrors can be used to dazzle people's eyes as well as to show what is actually there in front of them. Thus they can produce exactly contrary effects: they may either blind or reveal.

Love is provided with the same alternative. If the love is a bad love, there is blindness, and the light of God is not seen. Only passion — mutual passion, instead of mutual love — is reflected. If the love is a good love, there is the light of God to show the capacity for good that exists in those who stand before Him in charity. And it shows them also that the love that these bear toward one another is a reflection of love itself.

Although the effect of love is either to blind or to bring light, it would be a mistake to think of it as a temptation before we think of it as a revelation. It is a temptation only because man has made it so; in essence, it is what it always was. God granted the gift of love to man that man might reflect — come to look like — Him. The ideal still stands.

Sin, which is unlove, destroys the likeness of the soul to God. Love does not. Love does the exact opposite, compelling the soul toward resemblance, drawing it toward holiness, and burning up its contrary desires. Wrongly understood, love drags down and makes animalistic the instincts that were designed to sanctify. Rightly understood, love elevates and gives insight into what is confusing to the mind of man since the Fall.

The man who loves according to God learns more about himself than he ever guessed was there. He sees himself as he was originally, as he is essentially, and as he knows he always ought to be. His love gives him something to work upon in the way that he views the future. But more than this, the man who loves according to God begins to see what other people can become. His new appreciation of their value makes him long to devote himself to their — or to this particular one's — happiness. He sees that other people's happiness is more important than his own, and that their temporal and ultimate well-being must be his paramount concern. It is difficult to see how a man can ever come to know all this without love. Charity is man's supreme revelation.

The logical consequence of such knowledge is the desire to express it all in sacrifice. Love, human or divine, can lead to no other conclusion. The soul looks for a means of declaring itself that will be self-consuming. The soul forgets its own ambitions and is moved by the single ambition of self-surrender, self-giving. Charity teaches all about this.

The higher up the ladder of love the soul is drawn, the wider the horizon that opens out before it. Gratitude, sympathy, humility, compunction — qualities that never seemed to mean anything before — are now intuitively learned and become almost second nature. Charity is behind all of this.

∞

In ideal human love, self-love has no place

"But how is it that so often this is not the effect of love at all? If we are meant to find ourselves and others in human love, how is it that so many of us get lost in it and cause others to get lost? In the working out of love, is there not as much, if not more, greed than sacrifice? If the idea held out to man is really for universal acceptance, why are there so relatively few who even admit its validity — let alone try to live according to it?"

Anything — whether it be a principle or a Person — that is set for the fall or the resurrection of many[43] will have to be looked for. We do not come automatically upon the secrets of our happiness. If Christ's divinity lay hidden in His humanity, and if His sacramental presence comes to us under natural forms, we should expect to find a certain element of mystery about the composition of true love. As in the case of the Incarnation and the Blessed Sacrament, if we halt at the material element, we miss the substance of what is revealed.

As in all human things that relate to the divine, there has to be the act of faith. In faith we ask for the grace to know what we do not know by nature, to go on living according to an idea that transcends the ordinary habit of nature, to expect an ultimate confirmation of what can never be fully accounted for by nature.

Certainly there is mystery in love, but only a fraction of its problems has to do with lust. Lust, once detected as such, is a comparatively straightforward issue. Mysteries are seldom made

[43] Luke 2:34.

more difficult to grasp because of the heresies that are launched against them. In effect they are made more easy; the borderline doubts are cleared up. Lust may be the main practical obstacle to the realization of true love, but the trouble that eats away at the ideal is a combined self-deception, false romanticism, and dramatization.

A man who knows where he is with the love of God also knows where he is with blasphemy, sacrilege, and idolatry. Where he is not quite so sure is in matters of voluntary distraction during prayer, of the right attitude toward the letter of the law, and of vainglory. So a man who knows the place of human love in his soul also knows the place of lust in his soul. The difficulties come not so much with crude passion as with tender affection. Ill-regulated affection can get in where passion would not have a chance — and can do a great deal of harm.

Accept the highly plausible arguments in defense of non-vicious but romantic attachments, and you enter upon a sequence of evasions and substitutions. Harm is now done to the soul not only by the relationship itself, but also by the attitude of humbug that supports it.

To confront with a flat denial the excuses that both false reasoning and false advisers advance requires a high degree of faith and considerable tenacity of purpose. But it is the only way to the service of true love. It is a conflict, moreover, that is very sanctifying — sanctifying not only for the soul immediately involved in it, but also for the other who is the immediate cause of the conflict. Indeed, it is probably through this conflict, rather than through outward association, that the one soul is meant by God to benefit the other.

In this business of the heart, the effort to struggle against the demands of the flesh is seldom so wearing as the effort to respond to the ideals of the spirit. Fires flare up and are extinguished, but the consuming glow of a romantic attachment that cannot be seen as part of divine love, and which nevertheless cannot be quenched, may go on for years. And during those years, it may do either a great deal of good or a great deal of harm. It will lead either to God or to deeper self-deception and self-indulgence.

In the quest for an answer to the problems of human relationships, the mind and heart are tossed about and the soul is given no rest. If advice is asked, two opposite schools of thought declare themselves. The soul is thrown back upon itself, upon conscience, upon what it believes to be its call. Fearing to follow the promptings of the heart and unable, if only for practical reasons, to meet the sterner doctrine of separation, the soul nurses its trial in isolation. But nearly always this is just what God wants, just what He has been leading up to all along. He intends that the soul should feel cut off in this way so that He, and He alone, should be turned to for help. This is precisely the suffering that, at a given stage in the spiritual life, is judged by God to be more purifying than any other.

It is neither the solitude nor the turmoil that is the particular trial; the particular trial is having to go on loving in solitude. In the last analysis, it is loneliness that hurts us most. In this state, the soul knows that God is the only refuge and that, although the pull is all in the opposite direction, God must come first in love. The soul realizes, although obscurely and not experimentally as yet, that God is love itself. The soul sees that God may not be divided against Himself and that it is only the false apprehension of man that drives a wedge between divine and human love.

But although we may consent until our brains ache to the doctrine that God is love, and that the love that is not of God is no true love, we are thrown back in actual experience to an emotion that is terribly real — even if, according to the ideal, it is to be accounted as nothing. "If it is no part of the love of God," we say, "human love is nothing, is so much waste; and yet in my heart it is precisely human love that I find."

The soul knows that there is such a thing as ideal human love, and that if only things were different — if I were not made the way I am, if I had begun less selfishly, if I had been told about it more clearly from the beginning — it would be attainable. But at the same time, there is the feeling that, with the best desire in the world, this true love will in fact remain always out of reach. An agonizing contrast is now seen between the illimitable good that is held out to man and the wretched earthbound thing that is the present reality. Insofar as this painfully illuminating experience brings humility, it is a good. Certainly it is better than not knowing how wide is the gulf between the ideal and the actual. Still more is it better than knowing and pretending not to know.

So inexhaustible are the ramifications of self-deception that if the soul is to find union with God and with its fellowmen, there must be an unblinking fidelity to the light of truth. Even where the affections are not engaged at all, and where charity is more a matter of justice or duty or humanity than of love, there is quite a hideous amount of room for self. When we think we are finding our happiness in living for others, we may well be finding our happiness, or trying to, in living for self. Unless we seriously have God as the end of all our desire, the longing to do things for other people may well be only a longing for their gratitude or for their admiration. We hunger for approval, and if we are denied it from one direction, we make sure that we get it from another.

Giving things to those we love is often no more than giving to ourselves with even greater fidelity. When this happens, our friends are not our neighbors any longer; they are ourselves projected. When my neighbor is indistinguishable from me, my charity is indistinguishable from my self-love. I may want to do my neighbor good, but only because I want still more to do myself good.

Only when I want the good of God more than I want the good of anyone else or of myself can I be sure that I shall not come around again to my own good. And even then, there will be the need to grope my way and to keep pushing myself out of the path.

But at every stage, in this lifelong search for the right relationship between human beings, the belief must be maintained that such a relationship is possible. I must know that charity is there for the asking — if only I am content to wait upon God and not upon my own desires.

Just as, in order to be happy, I must believe in happiness, so, in order to love, I must believe in love. In order to be truly myself, I must believe that there is a self in me to whom it is worth being true. It is the same all along the line. In order to be just, merciful, and holy, I have to believe not only in justice, mercy, and holiness, but also in my capacity to respond to the graces of justice, mercy, and holiness. So, in order to have a part in true charity, I must be a believer in true charity: a believer in its source, its end, and in my place in its scheme. I must have hope and faith, therefore, if I am to love.

∞

Love of others develops from love of God

In order to see others in terms of God, then, and in order to render them true charity, I must believe that they are reflections of God and that they are on that account lovable. When I see what it is they reflect — *whom* it is they reflect — I may safely give love to the reflections. They then become a medium to me, and I to them, of the love of God.

But let there be no nonsense about this. A man must not reach out for his love of God and fit it artificially into his human relationships. God does not suffer Himself to be drawn in as an afterthought. The spiritual life does not exist to make natural instincts respectable. There must be no sleight of hand about placing our earthly affections in the scheme of God's service; it is only when the service of God comes incontestably first that the affections are seen to take their proper place.

So long as he seeks first the kingdom of God's love,[44] man may expect all these natural powers of his to assume due order. It is when he approaches love from the wrong end, with himself as the starting point, that he loses his way.

The man who allows God to be the pattern and purpose of his love need have no fear of being blinded by his love. The man who sees the type and the thing typified as coming from the same source has found the true perspective of his love.

[44] Cf. Matt. 6:33.

"He who lives in love lives in God, and God lives in him."[45] Those who truly give their hearts to God will find that God will come to rule them from within and will guide their loves. For then the affections will be no longer theirs but His. I love, now not I, but Christ loveth in me.[46]

[45] 1 John 4:16.
[46] Cf. Gal. 2:20.

Chapter Six

✺

Love God above all

If charity were directed in only the one direction, toward God, there would be no need to say more than what has just been said. Sanctity is charity and charity is sanctity, and this is as far as we can go. But because sanctity must embrace the whole of charity, and because charity has a twofold activity, we must consider how the love of God is to be developed in a way that includes and expresses the love of people.

In the previous chapter, we have dealt with human charity as the means by which we come to see souls as they are; love reveals to us their place in creation. The present chapter is concerned with love not as a means but as a perfection in its own right, and with the mistakes that can be made in the pursuit of this ideal.

Before we can be clear about what the principle is, we need to be clear about what it is not. Thus, man's affective nature does not have to be divided into two compartments: one concerned with God and the other with people; rather, his capacity for love has to be enlarged and directed so that it comes to resemble the activity possessed by God Himself. Just as God, in a single act, loves Himself and the reflection of Himself in human beings, so we must come to unify our love, seeing charity as the one principle of divine and human love. Not only is this idea enshrined for us in the Incarnation, but it is the Incarnation that makes such a divine-human love imitable.

The man who lives as a member of Christ's body, loves God and man with the love of Christ. In the union of charity, there can be no conflict of loves. God is love, and God is undivided. It is the division of operation that causes the difficulty.

The difficulty can be solved only by living up to the vocation of membership in Christ. When this is achieved, the soul begins to understand the full function of charity. Life lived on earth with other people, other reflections of God's love, is seen in unity. Where the wholeness of love is divided, you get false love. Not only do you get a false love competing with the true love of God, but ultimately you get a false note sounding in the love of God that might have remained true.

So deep is the wound inflicted upon the heart of man by Original Sin that, left to himself, he splits his loyalties and directs his affections along different channels. His only hope of getting his heart right with God and man is to model himself on the one Person who was both God and man.

In the family of God into which we are adopted, we perfect the harmony of brotherhood in the measure that we grow into the likeness of Christ our Brother. And in doing so, we perfect at the same time our filial relationship toward the Father. "Herein," says St. Leo in the fourth of his Nativity sermons, "is found the greatest of God's gifts: that man may call God his Father and Christ his Brother." And this greatest of God's gifts is nothing else but the wholeness of charity.

When all the members of the family make it their first purpose to fashion their characters according to the pattern of the one perfect member, the result is inevitably peace, unity, and charity. Those who have shaped their lives around the life of Christ must, by the practice of His charity, by the use of His gifts, and by obedience to His law and fidelity to His Gospel, grow into the sanctity that He has designed for the cells of the body of His love.

Sanctity is nothing else but living in such a union with God that our human relationships, our work, and our daily lives are informed by His Spirit, which is the Spirit of love. By cooperation with His mystical activity, exercised within our souls and without, we live by the power of grace and according to the gifts of the Holy Spirit. Our natures, under the action of divine love, are made one in Him. In both our outward and inward activity, the motive force is provided by the infused virtues — particularly the theological virtues[47] — while our affections derive their impulse from and obey the movements of charity.

The reconciliation of two apparently different principles of charity is explained, as fully as it is ever likely to be explained, by St. Paul in the thirteenth chapter of his first letter to the Corinthians. Grace and experience explain it, but it is not a doctrine that normally may be learned from books. It is the distinctive doctrine of St. John, among the Evangelists. But how many of us really come to incorporate it in our lives?

Every Christian soul should be able to see charity in terms of Christ, in terms of St. Paul's and St. John's teaching, and in terms of the source and end of all holiness. "With us," says St. Paul, "Christ's love is a compelling motive."[48] If we could say

---

[47] The theological virtues are faith, hope, and love, or charity.
[48] Cf. 2 Cor. 5:14.

the same, there would be no problem. The mystic, the saint, can mean St. Paul's words when he reads them because to him charity toward God is not so much the coefficient of his charitable acts toward men but the primary cause of all true human love. Charity is the compelling motive to action because without it, no action would be worthwhile.

"The charity of Christ urges us": it is at once the power and the attraction. When the power that moves the affections is not that of charity, there is division. It is the tragedy of love that it can turn against itself and commit suicide. Lust, by denying the origin and end of love, destroys its beauty.

Love is not lustful by nature, but it is imperfect by nature. It needs the grace of Christ's love if it is to keep its intended level. Otherwise it will drop from the supernatural to the natural, and from the natural to the lustful. "Christ," says St. Cyril of Alexandria,[49] "is the sanctifying power which gives perfection to the imperfect." It is as good for us to bear in mind how imperfect our affections are.

∞

Christ unites the members of His Body

Christ, who came that we "might have life and have it more abundantly,"[50] wills that the principle of that life be expressed and enjoyed corporately. Under the figure of the Good Shepherd, He preached the doctrine of collective unity;[51] under the figure of the vine, He preached the necessity of

---

[49] St. Cyril (died 444), Patriarch of Alexandria.

[50] Cf. John 10:10.

[51] John 10:14-16.

common reliance upon Him, the central stem;[52] under the figure of the cornerstone, He preached Himself as the sole support on which the separate elements of the house might safely rest.[53]

As the Bread of Life, He both assimilates the separate stalks of wheat and nourishes the individual members of His Church.[54] The parables abound in these symbols of common purpose. Christ leaves us in no doubt as to His desire, which is to weld together all the distinct identities of the human race and unite them to Himself so that they are transfigured into His likeness.

When we live by Him and in Him, we live lives of charity, member of member, bone of bone, with one another. Allowing us to live as members of His body, Christ imparts to each one the love with which He Himself loves.

Where love among the members is weak, the perfection of unity within the body is impaired. Where love is absent, the unity disintegrates. Where love is denied or desecrated or prostituted, there is no longer any show of harmony; there is confusion.

So long as souls exist in the harmony of mutual charity, they are loved by the Father with the love by which the Father loves the Son. They are animated by the Holy Spirit. When souls exclude themselves from the harmony of charity, they reject the Father's love, waste the merits of Christ's Passion, and expel the grace of the Holy Spirit at the same time.

[52] John 15:5-7.
[53] Matt. 21:42; Mark 12:10-11.
[54] John 6:35.

If, as St. Augustine[55] claims, souls are changed into Christ by means of the supernatural life He enables us to lead — "Admire and rejoice; we have become Christ, for He is the Head and we the limbs, and the whole makes up the living body, He and ourselves" — then, where the bond of unity is taken away, we change back again into what we were before, into nature.

∞

Human love calls for prudence

So much for the *theory* of charity. The question is how to translate this into action so that we may imitate the achievement of the early Christians who stood out from among their contemporaries as men who loved one another. "They had but one heart and one soul" says the Acts, and they held all things in common,[56] spiritual as well as temporal.

For man in his redeemed but still imperfect state, it is not easy, as we have seen, to keep the balance of charity. He tends not only to express one aspect of charity at the expense of the other, but, more grossly, to fail by either neglect or excess. Charity is probably more often offended against by an exaggeration of love than by a deficiency.

If it is an anomaly to scorn the love of one's neighbor on the grounds that the love of God is being well served, it is a travesty to worship one's neighbor on the grounds that all love comes from God and that one is therefore safe in going ahead with or without reference to Him who is the source. All affective

---

[55] St. Augustine (354-430), Bishop of Hippo.
[56] Cf. Acts 4:32.

desire does not come from God. It is only love in the strict sense that comes from God. Much that goes by the name of love is not from God at all, but from self, from corrupt desire.

The hurt done to charity by anger, envy, calumny, detraction — by all that we class as uncharity — is so obvious that it need not be discussed here. It is the harm done by private loves that have a color of charity but are not of charity that will have to be considered.

And it is not only because the directly uncharitable attitude appears as clearly reprehensible — instinct and common consent bearing witness against it — that its malice does not have to be further exposed; rather it is because the more subtle uncharities of inordinate attachments and too-tender affections are so often excused, and even canonized, that they need to be seen against the white light of the love of God.

To idealize the material beyond a certain point is humbug; to idealize it absolutely is idolatry. To sin against the first commandment, you do not have to worship a graven image; it is quite enough to put upon the highest pedestal a love that is not God's. The soul dedicated to the love and service of God must keep faithful to the ideal of exclusive possession by God. The whole heart has been handed over, and it must remain wholly handed over. To reclaim possession is to go back not only on a purpose but also on a Person.

St. John of the Cross states categorically that the love that is given to creatures by an interior soul is love taken away from God. By this he manifestly does not mean that the love of benevolence is wrong, because this is sheer charity, but he must surely mean that the *amor amicitiae* ("the love of friendship") must be very clearly proved free of *amor concupiscentiae* ("the love of desire") if it is not to be found taking away from the *amor Dei soli* ("the love of God alone"). God is not merely first among those who attract us. He places Himself before us as the object of our whole desire.

If, having assented to this proposition and directed our wills toward Him and Him alone, we find that our affections are still engaged — as they very well may be, since they cannot be altogether controlled — there is no infidelity to grace. There is infidelity only when we encourage, or cling to, an attachment whose origin and end is not in God.

To feel sensibly attracted is not wrong; it may not be avoided. To follow up that attraction with a view to finding satisfaction in it would be wrong; it would mean a diversion of the way that is designed to lead straight to God.

To experience the emotion of deep human love in one's life is not wrong. Indeed, it is right, for there is nothing that reveals human life to us so immediately as human love. But it would be wrong to pursue the element of uncontrollable desire that is connected with deep human love.

To enjoy the mutual understanding and security of friendship is not wrong; friendship is frequently blessed in Holy Scripture. Love between man and woman, moreover, is hallowed by the dignity of a sacrament. There is nothing wrong with love as such — quite the contrary. It is the passion that we inherit from the Fall that merits all these qualifications and demands all these safeguards. It is passion, in the sense of corrupt desire, that spoils the beauty of what might otherwise be safe as well as holy.

Emotions that are disciplined and in constant subjection to the impulse of grace are stronger and deeper and nobler than those that know no law. The moral and mystical power of a mind trained in self-abnegation comes to reinforce the activity of love, not to vitiate it.

To surrender to human love may well touch a deep level of human experience, but there is nothing particularly heroic about this. No significant human values are learned by indulgence. But on the other hand, to triumph over passion is to mount to a level of nobility in which the realities of human experience speak for themselves.

So it is not by yielding to desire nor by trying to eliminate desire — still less by lending a top-dressing of artificial idealism to desire — that the soul is to find its answer to the problem of love. It will find the answer only in transformation and repeated redirection.

As a symbol of this you have, traced through the sequence of the *Divine Comedy*, Dante's romantic love for Beatrice, which begins in nature and ends in the spirit.[57] So our human loves must, if they are to go by the sacred name of love at all, be purified in the *Inferno* and *Purgatorio* of ascetic practice until in *Paradiso*, they are transfigured into the selflessness of the love of God.

---

[57] In his allegorical poem the *Divine Comedy*, Dante Alighieri (1265-1321; Italian poet and philosopher) is led by his beloved Beatrice on a journey through Hell (the *Inferno*), Purgatory (*Purgatorio*), and Heaven (*Paradiso*).

Chapter Seven

Find union with God in the Eucharist

It is a common mistake to confuse the virtue of religion with the love of God. The two may express themselves in the same way, but they are not the same thing. The love of God carries the soul beyond the exercise of the service of God. The virtue of religion is concerned with means; the love of God is an end in itself.

Whereas the virtue of religion relates to the worship due to God, the virtue of divine charity relates to God Himself. Thus, to imagine that the service of God is the whole story is to think of the effect, instead of the principle that gives value to the effect. Service may never be allowed to take the place of love; love is both the inspiration and end of service.

Ideally speaking, the virtue of religion and the virtue of charity should develop proportionately, should act as one. The whole function of religion is ultimately to further homage done in love. But in practice, it is difficult to maintain the balance: we can err either by restricting the virtue of religion to the *forms* of religion or by denying charity the need for external expression. The corrective to both these misconceptions is provided in the Holy Eucharist.

The Holy Eucharist not only develops, defines, and comes as the consummate expression of the virtue of religion, but also actively increases in the soul the possession of love itself. With the access of sanctifying grace, the sanctity of the soul is advanced by Holy Communion to a degree that no other works performed in virtue of religion could achieve. The reason for this is that the sanctity of the soul is measured not by works of religion but by love.

It is true that sanctity shows itself in the practice of the virtues, and that this supposes outward acts of religion, but it is also true that, whereas virtuous behavior needs love as its motive, the motive of love is love itself. The Holy Eucharist is the sacrament of love.

Theologians distinguish between *perfectio substantialis* in the soul and *perfectio simpliciter*. They tell us that where there is no mortal sin, there is a substantial perfection: there are grounds for a further perfection, and the soul is at least perfectly alive. The other kind of perfection, considered simply as sanctity, is the plenitude to which earnest souls feel called to aspire. The Holy Eucharist ministers to each of these perfections: in the first instance, the soul is actively helped to keep itself in a state of grace; in the second, its horizons of love are enlarged. If love is the "bond of perfection"[58] and the Holy Eucharist is the sacrament of love, then Holy Communion not only draws together outward behavior and inward motive but also raises *perfectio substantialis* toward *perfectio simpliciter*.

Experience shows, however, that charity can grow cold. Even those who frequently receive Holy Communion may

[58] Col. 3:14.

find themselves failing in the love of God. Evidence, exterior as well as interior, may prove that the deterioration is not merely something supposed by an oversensitive conscience, but is something real. What then? How is it that the eucharistic life has ceased to vivify the life of love, the life of the spirit?

Where the conditions are not fulfilled, there is no guarantee that the effects will be produced. Frequent Communion is not magic; the downward tendency of fallen nature is still to be accounted for. The Holy Eucharist does not, as if by a charm, bend an ill-disposed character so that, in spite of itself, the soul finds itself rising to the heights.

Although in the natural order there are such things as warm springs, water is, in the ordinary way, cold. If hot water is wanted, it has to be heated, and when the heat is taken away, it begins to get cold again. It does not get hot all at once, nor does it get cold all at once. If you want a steady level of hot water, you have to give it a steady pressure of heat. And the water will not maintain its temperature, however steady the flame underneath it, if cold water is constantly being added.

Occasionally you get souls that are naturally fervent, that are like warm springs; but in the ordinary way, the soul tends to coldness. The soul has to be heated up with the pressure of grace, and if the pressure is removed, the soul grows first tepid and then stone cold. The soul cannot expect to be anything but lukewarm without the grace of frequent Holy Communion, and if Holy Communion is neglected for any length of time, the heat goes out of the soul altogether. Nor can the soul, however frequent its reception of the Holy Eucharist, expect to increase in the love of God if cold water is being allowed to come in and reduce the temperature.

Although it is the nature of the Holy Eucharist to promote the love of God and the virtue of religion, its action is conditioned by the willingness of the recipient. If the recipient opens his soul to influences that are alien to the influence of grace — that is, if he tolerates habits of sin — he stifles the good he should be receiving.

Given a certain stimulus and environment, an oyster will produce a pearl; take away the particular conditions, and no oyster will produce a pearl. You may open a thousand oysters and find no pearl, but you will know that a pearl might well have been found in any one of them. From one Holy Communion, a soul may derive the grace to become a saint. The fact that a thousand Communions do not produce sanctity makes no difference to the plenitude of love and grace that is contained in the Holy Eucharist.

∞

God desires union with you

It is God's will that the life of man should be the eucharistic life: "Believe me when I tell you this: you can have no life in yourselves unless you eat the flesh of the Son of Man and drink His blood."[59] It remains His will even when men decide to reject this life.

God wills that all men should attain to union with Him. The union of souls with Him remains His will even though countless souls may reject the opportunity and oppose His will. Our life depends upon the Holy Eucharist; our union with God depends upon the Holy Eucharist. For the Catholic,

[59] Cf. John 6:54 (RSV = John 6:53).

be he mystic or weekly-Mass parishioner, there is no religion apart from eucharistic religion and no life that is not fed by the Bread of Life.

Religion, then, is seen as love, life as love, and sanctity as love. Charity not only fulfills the law in the sense of keeping the whole of it, but informs the law. That is to say, it gives life to service. When charity possesses the soul as it is meant to possess it, the relationship between the soul and God goes beyond duty and justice. The virtue of religion is now no longer the yoke of divine love; it is one with divine love.

Love is God's gift to us in the Holy Eucharist. This is because God is love and He gives Himself to us. When we read that our Lord "loved His own to the end,"[60] we are to understand not only that He loved His own until the end of His life but, more significant, to the furthest possible limit. He could not have given to man a greater gift than that which was love itself. In Holy Communion, we receive the All. God in His entirety comes to man.

Thus, in communicating Himself to man, God realizes to the fullest degree His love for His creatures. What other explanation could there be for His wanting to remain with us in the Blessed Sacrament, for His wanting to visit our human bodies in Holy Communion, for His desire that we should live in Him and by Him? Love, as well as being the gift itself, is the only explanation of the gift.

There can be no further consummation of our Lord's purpose in relation to the soul on earth than that which is found in the sacrament of the Holy Eucharist. Thus He comes not

---

[60] Cf. John 13:1.

only so that our love should be fed, but so that His should be fulfilled. It is as much His expression of desire as our expression of response.

It is not as though we first loved Him, but that He loved us.[61] Once we grasp this essential truth in our relationship with God, we come to see deeper and deeper into the mysteries of religion, deeper and deeper into the workings of grace. We begin to glimpse something of the Providence of God which elicits our absolute dependence and surrender, something of the mercy of God which makes us never hesitate to ask for pardon for ourselves and for others, something of the way in which even our own prayers and sacrifices are not our gifts to Him, but are much more His gifts to us. And the living evidence of this truth, the symbol that should remind us of it every day, is the Holy Eucharist.

The Incarnation did not begin and end at a certain moment in time, leaving the future of mankind to benefit by its single act; its work is continued in the Blessed Sacrament. Although this is true of the Blessed Sacrament that is reserved in the tabernacle, it is all the more true of the Blessed Sacrament that is received into the body and soul of man. The benefits of the Incarnation reach their fullest expression in Holy Communion.

It is the same with the application of the merits of Calvary. Although the work of the Redemption is realized in the reconciliation of all mankind in general to the Father, it is when the redemptive act of Christ is re-enacted in the Sacrifice of the Mass, and when Christ Himself is received at this eucharistic

---

[61] 1 John 4:10.

representation of Calvary, that Christ's love for man reaches its climax.

It is not only that we need the merits of the Incarnation and the Redemption; it is that Christ's love is so great that He needs us for the perfection of its activity. It is not that we are necessary to God — that would mean that He was dependent upon His creatures — but that we, although finite, are required to be objects of a love that is infinite. There can be no greater love than that which is proved by Christ's laying down His life for man.[62]

Therefore, when Christ, in His substantial body, incarnate as He was in the womb of Mary, comes to us in Holy Communion under the appearance of bread and wine, He is answering His own longing as well as stimulating a longing for Himself in us.

∞

God is the source of all
your prayer and spiritual effort

In our foolishness, in our muddleheaded humility, we instinctively wonder what it can be that draws the divine desire to such unworthy objects as ourselves. The answer is simply that what He sees in us is the likeness that we bear to Him. And since with every reception of the Holy Eucharist, we can come nearer to reproducing this likeness, He desires that we should receive Him as often as possible.

It is only God who can be at the same time the subject and object of desire. We, by responding to the grace that this desire

---

[62] John 15:13.

imparts to us, both further His purpose by way of object and at the same time bring to Christ, the subject, the maximum of praise and love that man is capable of rendering.

Thus, the love that we bring to Christ in the Holy Eucharist is not so much ours as His. And because it is His, it is so much more effective and meritorious than anything we ourselves could provide. We have nothing; He gives us everything. It is His wish that, in Holy Communion, all the merits of His humanity, all the virtue attached to the various stages of His earthly existence, should be applied to the soul of the communicant.

We are inclined to imagine, as we make our preparation for or thanksgiving after receiving Communion, that the force of our prayer, although aided, of course, by grace, comes from ourselves. We assume that, whether praying for what we want with the prayer of petition or praying for what God wants with the prayer of surrender, it is we who are doing the greater part of the work, and that it is due to our industry and imagination that we are finding suitable forms of self-expression. The mystics would have us look at the matter differently.

To return to the simile already used, the comparison of heating up water, the mystics would show that to one who had never seen boiling water before, the bubbles on the surface might well appear to be the cause of the water's heat; the bubbles seem so much more dynamic than either the steady, silent flame that burns underneath or the cool, thin wire that carries the electricity. In our prayers, on the occasions when we see anything at all, we see only the bubbles.

Explaining how prayers of petition that are answered do not change the mind of God, but have all along been elicited from us by grace, Dionysius[63] compares the soul to a sailor pulling on a rope that is held fast to a rock. To the sailor in his boat, the rock looks as if it is coming toward him in answer to his effort. But in fact the rock, like the will of God, is immovable. We pray, not so as to change the mind of God, but so as to obtain from Him the good that He wants us to have on condition that we ask for it.

To expand Dionysius's idea, taking it beyond the prayer of petition and applying it to prayer in general, it could be said that the rope that is put into our hands is not one of our own making or selection, but is the one chosen for the purpose by God. It may be rough to handle; it may slip through our fingers; it may appear to be hopelessly unequal to the task of pulling us to shore. But it is the only one we can use at the moment, and we must be content with it.

Not only has the rope been put into our hands by God, but the strength with which we are able to pull is equally His gift. This strength, because it is love, is developed by nothing as much as by the Holy Eucharist. If we hope to keep up the steady pull of love, we need to be living the eucharistic life to our fullest capacity. The rope is no good if it is not pulled; prayer is no good if there is no love.

So whether we are considering sanctity as a whole, or prayer and the Holy Eucharist more particularly, we have to recognize before all else the source of our inspiration and our effort — not only the source but the term. God is the Alpha and the Omega, the first and the last, the beginning and the

---

[63] Possibly Dionysius the Pseudo-Areopagite (c. 500), mystical theologian. — ED.

end.[64] We try to become holy, we try to pray, we try to live the full eucharistic life, not only because of our own ideas of perfection, but also because of His.

Our success in this business of drawing nearer to the rock that is Christ is measured not by our ideas of navigation, not by the skill with which we manipulate the rope, and not even by rough weather we may meet on the way, but by love. So what we must do is to look not at the rope or at ourselves, and still less at the waves that threaten, but at the rock. True love forgets itself in the outgoing movement toward the object of its love.

If the plenitude of human life is to be found in the eucharistic life fully lived, then sanctity and prayer and the service of God need no further explanation; God is charity, and charity is the bond of perfection. Once the soul learns the meaning of love, as all souls are intended to learn in the unfolding of their eucharistic relationship with God, there is nothing more to worry about.

But do we ever really learn? Perhaps it is none but the greatest saints who have no further need to examine themselves as to how they are placed in relation to the virtues other than charity, to the gifts of the Holy Spirit, to the traditional practices of devotion and religion. For us who are not saints, who dare not assume that "the charity of Christ urges us"[65] at every moment of the day and in every decision we must make, there are steps to be mounted and means to be employed.

The Holy Eucharist, at once the means and the end, enables us daily to deepen the sense of St. Paul's words: "I live,

[64] Rev. 22:13.
[65] Cf. 2 Cor. 5:14.

now not I, but Christ liveth in me."[66] Uniting everything that is perfect into one — namely, Himself — Christ gives this to us in the name of love. Life becomes love, and love becomes life. The human being abides in the divine, and the divine in the human being. The share that by Baptism we have in the life of God becomes, with the grace of the Holy Eucharist, closer. "As the Father hath sent me, and I live by the Father, so he that eateth me the same shall live by me."[67]

Christ is the only way to the Father, and those who see Christ see the Father also.[68] Those who are nourished by Christ's body are at the same time extending the graces that flow from the indwelling of the Father and the Holy Spirit. The Blessed Sacrament is not a mystery that separates itself from the Trinity in Heaven and comes down to earth for the love of man. The Blessed Sacrament is Christ, and Christ is God, and God is undivided.

It is when a man discovers Christ that he discovers the Father and the Holy Spirit. It is also then that he discovers love and discovers himself.

So permeated are we by the egotism left to us by the Fall that it is only when the principle of our lives is God and not self that we come to be our true identities. And it is just then that we do not bother any more about who those true identities may be. Love is self-forgetting. Love looks only to the beloved. The Holy Eucharist is the sacrament of love.

[66] Gal. 2:20.
[67] John 6:58 (RSV = John 6:57).
[68] Cf. John 14:6, 9.

Chapter Eight

Love God's will

The most common error people make about the service of God is to imagine that sanctity has eluded them and that there exist no reasonable grounds for believing that it should ever come their way again. "And even if it should come my way again," they say, "the demands would be too great; I am not as generous as I was." In other words, they are looking at the grace of sanctity as though it were a painted horse on a merry-go-round: you hop on before the pace gets too fast, or else you miss your chance altogether.

"I have never produced any but the most insignificant works for God," they say, "and I am not likely to produce anything more significant now." But for sanctity, it is not bigger works that have to be produced, but better works.

For the production of better (as distinct from greater) works, you do not have to go out of your way to prepare an environment. What you have to do is perfect the environment that is yours. And this does not mean shaping the existing order into a preconceived mold of holiness; it means shaping your own desires so that they fit exactly into the mold of the existing order. The fewer the references to preconceived molds of holiness, whether considered as a setting for the perfect service of

God or as a particular kind of personal perfection, the better. "The word of God is not bound";[69] sanctity can spring up any-where, in the most unlikely of settings and in the most un-likely of people

Even so, even allowing that the whole stuff of sanctity is nothing other than the deepening and extending of "not my will but Thine be done,"[70] we are nevertheless sadly aware of our inadequacy in the face of sanctity's demand. We feel we are not equipped by nature, nor yet by grace, to meet the chal-lenge of the love of God.

But may not this be because we have false ideas both of the will of God and the love of God? If we can have preconceived ideas about ourselves and about sanctity, we can certainly have preconceived ideas that are equally wrong about the will and love of God. The more freely terms are used, the more confused their meanings tend to become, and we can apply to the terms "will of God" and "love of God" connotations that, if not false, are at least artificial.

From knowing more or less the kinds of things that our own wills do, we judge that God's will must operate along roughly similar lines; having ourselves experienced love toward others, we think of God's love as being our own, stretched out to infinity. It is perfectly natural to make such deductions, simply because we naturally turn to ourselves for our terms of reference, but it is misleading.

To infer from my own outbursts of temper that the anger of God is an emotion like mine, only infinitely more intense, is

[69] 2 Tim. 2:9.
[70] Luke 22:42.

to draw a false conclusion. Yet there must be an analogy, or I would not read in Scripture about the wrath of God.[71] The truth is that my own anger is a symbol of something in God that I do not fully understand but that I know enough about to see that it leads to the punishment of my sins.

Instinctively I think of the mercy of God as the sudden melting of an attitude that was intended to be stern; of the Providence of God as the planning on the part of an infinitely comprehensive mind that must prepare for an infinite variety of eventualities; and of the generosity of God as the dealing out of gifts from an inexhaustible store. If I thus tend to mistake the nature of those divine qualities, the benefits of which I experience as the occasion arises, I must take all the more care not to mistake the will and love of God, which touch me all day long.

Yet it is not strictly a matter of taking care or making an effort. I can make a goodwill advance toward trying to understand the attributes of God, but it will be the light received in prayer that will show me the meaning of what I know so imperfectly in their operations.

Grace alone can bring God's mysteries nearer to me, and until it explains God's ways to me, my vision, even aided by the truths of revelation and the theology of the Church, is wretchedly incomplete. For years, thinking that I understand them, but in fact seeing only a glimmering of their effects, I can fumble about among forms, and then, when the light of the life of prayer has begun to penetrate into my being, I discover that the spiritual astigmatism from which I have been

[71] John 3:36; Rom. 1:18.

unconsciously suffering all along has been corrected. I can judge the things of God now by faith rather than by sense and feeling. Material modes of apprehension drop away, and I am given to worship in spirit and in truth.

∞

God enables you to desire and seek His will

When we bear this in mind, the knowledge of the will and love of God takes on a new perspective. The will of God, correctly but inadequately understood as representing the decrees of divine authority intermittently expressed and covering all temporal contingencies, is now felt to be a force operating within and not only from without, as before.

Where hitherto the soul had come by industry and habit to recognize in each circumstance as it came along the signified will of God, now it finds itself living in the will of God and recognizing circumstances as forming part of it.

When called upon to meet a suffering, the soul feels less inclined to say, "This is bearable because it must be the will of God, however obscurely it reveals itself as such to me," and more inclined to say, "God's will is my will, so, since He wants this, I do also."

The formula "the will of God" is a great help as a reminder, but it is better to think of it as God unceasingly willing than as a separate piece of God's will.

To unite myself with the will of God, I do not have to step outside my own will and lie down under His — as if the steamroller of "God's will" had to flatten me out; rather, I have to develop an awareness of what is going on all the time. Here inside me I can "accept" the will of God at every moment.

When we pray that God's will may be done on earth as it is in Heaven,[72] we are praying not that some secret will of God may declare itself to man — may drop, as it were, from Heaven to earth — but that the evident will of God may be seen and obeyed in the souls and lives of men. God's will is something that cannot help but be done; the whole question for us is how far we conform to it: "Thine immutable will be done on earth by us freely."

We may pray that God's will declare itself in this or that way, but our petitions do not change the mind of God. His will does not change to suit this or that emergency. Both the emergency and its solution are in the will of God, and He has inspired the prayers that go up to Him for the particular fulfill-ment of His will. When our prayers are answered in the sense of our petitions, it is not that we have succeeded, by the inten-sity of our faith, in bending God's will so that it coincides with our own; it is rather that God, through the channel of the faith He has given us, is doing His own will in our souls.

A child may ask his father for a particular present and may get it, but if the father's intention all along has been to give the present on the condition that he is asked for it, it would be wrong to say that the father is doing the child's will. On the contrary, the child is doing the father's will.

The answers we receive to our requests in prayer are not as though drawn from a stock of unappropriated favors and be-stowed upon us as rewards for merit. They are what God has seen to be the solution to our particular need, and their bestowal has been made dependent upon our request. It is

[72] Matt. 6:10.

not so much that the good things we ask for are dropped from Heaven, released by our petition, as that they come to us in the wisdom of God's Spirit, which is His will, working through us and by us and in us.

∞

God's will surrounds you

Only when I can say with Christ, "My will is to do always the will of my heavenly Father"[73] can I say that I have found what I am looking for. Until then, until I am emptied of self-interest and made obedient to the Father's will with the obedience of Christ, I am searching. That is why I shall have to go on searching all my life. In Heaven it will be different. To be doing always the will of the heavenly Father is the precise bliss of Heaven. But for as long as earthly life lasts, the search lasts.

The search is at least made easier by the knowledge that the will of the heavenly Father, although to be fulfilled imperfectly by me, is lying everywhere at hand. I cannot escape the will of God even if I want to. When, like a Jonah or a Balaam, I run away from the will of God,[74] I am caught up and made to see that I have been in it the whole time. "If I ascend into Heaven, Thou art there; if I go down into the depths, Thou art present. If I take my wings early in the morning and dwell in the uttermost parts of the sea, even there also shall Thy hand lead me."[75]

[73] Cf. John 8:29.
[74] Jon. 1:3; Num. 22:20-22.
[75] Ps. 138:8-10 (RSV = Ps. 139:8-10).

As unavoidable as water to the fish, as air to the bird, the will of God meets me at every point in my life. It is in my lungs, and I live by it. I do not have to wait for evidence of God's will to appear; the will itself is here, waiting for me to submit to it.

People tell me to "see God's will" in the commands of those in authority, in humiliations, in sickness, and in the loss of friends. But better than seeing God's will as occasions, as if standing in a queue to be hailed by me in their ordered sequence, is seeing it as an abiding summons within my soul — not as successive pressures, but as a continued presence.

This is why sanctity consists not in enlarging the scope of the work we do for God, but in improving its character. This is why, in order to find sanctity and peace and true liberty, we do not have to break out of the mold in which our lives are cast. All we have to do is surrender ourselves to God's will.

Sanctity is allowing ourselves to become increasingly assimilated into the will of God, which is increasingly seen to be the love of God, which is increasingly seen to be God Himself. There is nothing here about forcing a pattern holiness or framing a conditioned environment. Love is independent of patterns and environments, and ultimately the whole thing turns on the question of love.

"Love of God," "God's love for man": these are more phrases that have to be learned in God's sense rather than in ours. What we have considered in connection with His will might almost stand as applied to His love. The terms are virtually convertible: it is the association of a separate operation that makes for the distinction. The expressions of God's will are explained by God's love; the expressions of His love are to be received as His will. God is one; His will does not differ from His inspiration. And His inspiration, His Spirit, is love.

That Christ meant us to see the relation between the will and the love of God is shown by what He said to those who told Him that His mother and brothers were waiting for Him. "Behold my mother and my brothers. For whosoever shall do the will of God, of my Father who is in Heaven, he is my brother and my sister and my mother."[76]

It means, then, that God loves us in working His will among us, and that we love Him in cooperating.

It means that every apparent contradiction we must suffer is a sign of His love, and that every submission to it is a sign of ours.

It means that every time we unite ourselves with His will against our own self-will, we unite ourselves with His love against our own self-love.

It means that my aim from one point of view is to know, love, and do God's will, and from another, to will nothing else but God's love. When I have made God's love the whole object of my desire, I shall be happy. To want God's will and to do it, to want God's love and to respond to it: this is the purpose of my existence; apart from it, my life has no significance whatever.

"But *has* it no significance? Suppose that God's love for you prompts a genuine call to the missions or to work in extreme poverty, and you decide to follow a religious but less heroic vocation. Is not your life of the least significance? Is not God being served, and are not you being saved?"

---

[76] Cf. Mark 3:34-35.

This is where we have to distinguish between what theologians call God's *antecedent will* and His *consequent will*. Antecedently, God may have willed me to be a missionary, but, on my rejection of this particular grace, He has willed consequently that I should make a success of the vocation that in fact I have come to choose.

God's will, antecedent and consequent, never ceases to be my holiness. "This is the will of God: your sanctification."[77] Although not at the height of its original possibility, God's will for me, consequent now, remains an effective will; the vocation I have chosen to follow remains a vocation; the graces that are measured to my present, and objectively less perfect, state remain graces. The injunction "Be you perfect as your heavenly Father is perfect"[78] still stands.

Although objectively I am in a lower way of love than I might be, subjectively I am nevertheless within reach of high perfection. It is consoling to reflect that I shall be judged not by the heights to which, under other circumstances, I might have attained, but by the love with which I have performed the works of my actual condition of life.

So it amounts to this: the principle about doing and loving God's will holds good, and the only thing that has changed as the result of choosing the less perfect way is the field of its application. We are back again to the question of environment, which we have judged to be accidental only, and not essential to the work of sanctification. To choose the less perfect of two ways is still to choose a way that may — indeed, must — be

[77] 1 Thess. 4:3.
[78] Matt. 5:48.

made perfect. The fact that it is less perfect than perfection is all the more reason why it should be made more perfect than imperfection.

Extending by analogy the terminology of the theologians, we might say of divine love that, as in the case of the divine will, there is an antecedent and consequent activity. The purpose of God's antecedent love in my regard can act as my inspiration; His consequent love is my immediate necessity. Thus, I would like to have been more generous in my response when the initial offer was open; I want to live at the level to which in the mind of God I belong; I accept the state in which I find myself, and whatever the degree of my love, I mean it to be the highest of which I am capable.

If this represents my attitude, I shall find that, far from being conditioned by my environment, I shall be conditioning it. There is never any need for a man to become the creature of circumstance, but, in order to become master of circumstance, he will need the light of grace to know about the will and love of God.

It is the inner and not the outer life that qualifies. Those things that enter into a man from without do not defile a man. Nor do they sanctify him. The things that defile and sanctify are the things that are in the heart of a man, and that come out of him.[79]

To conclude: Sanctity creates its environment as it goes along; sin creates its environment as it goes along. The point of departure is the will of man, not the pressure of creatures. And the will of man must follow the will and love of God, not

[79] Mark 7:15.

the law and love of creatures. When the will of man does this, it is secure; to follow the other way is unhappiness and death.

It is when the soul has set out either toward God or toward self that environment plays its contributive part. The things that God has made good may be turned to bad use, and the things that man has made bad may be brought back again to good.

Thus, to return to the opening paragraph of this chapter, it is a cardinal error for souls to imagine that sanctity has eluded them and that the existing setting of their lives makes it unlikely that they would respond if the opportunity were to come again.

Chapter Nine

∞

Strive to purify your soul

Sanctity is not penance,[80] and penance is not sanctity; but sanctity seeks to express its spirit in penance, and penance seeks to find its fulfillment in sanctity.

The man who feels drawn to do penance need not imagine, in spite of the warnings that come to him from many directions, that he is in the wrong way of spirituality. He may possibly not be in the right way, but if this is the case, it will not be because of his attraction to penance. To judge from the way people talk and write, you would suppose that to be moved to do penance was something discreditable, and that there could be only one motive for the desire, namely, vainglory.

A soul is certainly liable to go wrong by attaching too much importance to acts of penance and not enough to the other aspects of the service of God, but a soul is also liable to go wrong if any one aspect is exaggerated at the expense of the rest. You do not have to wait until you experience the urge to

[80] By *penance*, Dom van Zeller means acts of self-denial and reparation that help atone for sin, purify the soul, and turn man away from sin. See also Dom Hubert van Zeller, *Spirit of Penance, Path to God* (Manchester, New Hampshire: Sophia Institute Press, 1998). — ED.

do penance before you have a chance of becoming either a freak or a heretic.

Penance is not merely fasting, and fasting is not necessarily penance; but just as sanctity seeks to express itself in penance, so penance often seeks to express itself in fasting. Just as devout souls can, in the name of religion, become so absorbed in external works of charity as to lose touch with the essence of charity, so also can devout souls become absorbed in the externals of penance. When they do this, they lose touch with the essence of penance.

The combination of vanity and a too-natural zeal can undermine both charity and penance. Vanity and zeal look to the exterior; charity and penance, to the interior. The value of a soul's exterior works is measured by that soul's interior sanctification. "An act is so much the more meritorious," says St. Thomas,[81] "when the grace that informs it is greater." Thus, when the outward act is impelled by a human motive, it can be judged only by human standards. Not until grace informs our acts — that is, not until we have formed a supernatural motive — can we expect our acts to merit supernaturally.

If, then, our acts are pleasing or displeasing to God according to the will with which they are performed, it is of primary importance that our outward acts of charity and penance are launched with a supernatural motive.

Even putting worldly motives aside, we can be actuated in our virtuous works by impulses that are good but not good enough. The desire to accumulate merit is one such motive;

---

[81] St. Thomas Aquinas (c. 1225-1274), Dominican philosopher and theologian.

the fear of incurring blame for tepidity is another. Souls can be greedy for spiritual standing just as they can be greedy for social or intellectual standing. When the ambition is spiritual, there is all the more need to see that it springs from a strictly spiritual impulse.

If, again, penance were simply the product of servile fear, it would have no place in the life of the saint whose life is ruled by the love that casts out fear.[82] But there is still the fear that is filial, which is a combination of humility and a dread of giving offense, and the love of God is not meant to cast this out. The love of God increases it, and its expression is penance.

Without the right kind of fear, a man cannot even begin to be wise, since "fear is the beginning of wisdom."[83] And without the right kind of penance, a man cannot find an outlet for either his fear or his love. The wisdom he will acquire from his fear and his love will teach him what form his penance is to take.

In suggesting above that penance ordinarily chooses the discipline of fasting, we are advancing the traditional exercise; from the earliest times, the faithful have been exhorted to this particular mode of reparation and love. The Church has sanctified the practice, and the saints have borne witness to its benefits.

But apart from the historical justification of fasting, there is a symbolic and psychological fitness about going without food that is not found to the same extent in the case of other mortifications. The hunger of the soul is reflected in the hunger of

---

[82] 1 John 4:18.
[83] Cf. Ps. 110:10 (RSV = Ps. 111:10); Prov. 1:7.

the body; the dependence of the soul upon the power of grace is reflected in the body's weakness when deprived of its ordinary nourishment.

So it is nothing unusual when souls experience an intense longing to fast. At a certain stage, it is the physical and psychological counterpart of a spiritual development. Subject always to obedience, the soul that feels drawn to fasting should follow the attraction and make the most of it while health and work allow.

Experience shows that God rewards the desire to fast by giving to those who are generous in this matter additional powers of endurance. And it is not only that a man will find himself able to manage on a small quantity of food, but that his mind is keener because of the practice, and that his whole spiritual purpose is made increasingly alive to him. If eating a lot is liable to blunt the sensibilities, eating little is liable to sharpen the appetite for the more serious things of life. Certainly the more serious things of religion are more deeply valued when one is hungry than when one is not.

The mind, purified by fasting, is not only more eager to take on other penitential practices, but, trained in detachment from the most immediate satisfactions of sense, such a mind is more able to judge the relative usefulness of the possible penances to be adopted.

If the same penances were found to produce the same benefits in all souls, there would be no difficulty. But each man has to weigh his own temperament, his attraction, his strengths, and his weaknesses. This he will do before God in prayer. If he does not do this before God in prayer, he will find himself doing it before his own vanity in the mirror.

It is good to remember, while choosing penances, that some are to be taken up for a time only and then dropped. This is not to leave the door open to instability; it is to ensure that the particular mortifications in question do their work. The body so soon gets used to some mortifications that, unless intervals in the observance are allowed, the effect will be virtually lost. The body never gets used to hunger and want of sleep, however.

∞

Fear can hinder your willingness to do penance

The excuses people make for their neglect of the duty of voluntary penance fall roughly under three heads. (Laziness is not an excuse; it is an explanation.)

First, it is advanced that interior mortifications are far more valuable than exterior mortifications, and that if one takes care to curb the imagination and the passions, one is satisfying one's obligation. The answer to this is that of course it is better to mortify the mind than the body, but the point is that a man should mortify both. It is not left to the individual to choose between correcting mental or physical indulgence; he is expected, if he has set himself to search for perfection in the service of God, to deny himself all along the line.

By denying himself the satisfaction of physical appetites, and by imposing a measure of hardship upon himself, a man trains his senses so that they are more ready to respond to the obedience placed over them by the will. This means that when the whole man, sense and spirit, is called upon to meet a crisis, he will not be greatly distracted by the rebellion of the flesh; he will be used to subduing it.

Furthermore it is by generosity in the practice of exterior penance, which is admittedly inferior to interior penance, that the soul shows to God and to itself that it is willing to welcome occasions of interior mortification when they present themselves. Your custody of the eyes[84] is a token offering, showing your readiness to practice custody of the heart. Abstaining from reading newspapers and listening to the radio denotes the intention of turning away from the affairs of the world and fixing your whole attention upon God.

The second reason people give for rejecting the thought of voluntary penance takes the following form: "Why try to improve upon the penances that are sent by God — particularly when the voluntary kind is seen to result in intolerance and vanity?"

The function of voluntary penance is not to be a *substitute* for necessary penance, but, as we have seen in the case of the earlier objection, to support it. The sufferings chosen for us by God are always more wisely chosen than our self-chosen mortifications. The question is, shall we choose to suffer His if we never choose our own?

As to vanity's being the most immediate effect of self-inflicted austerity, the distinction should be made between what is immediately perceptible and what is fundamentally significant. It is up to each soul, with the help of a director, to see whether the incidental effects outweigh the essential good. Self-denial is a good; it is designed to produce good in the soul.

---

[84] "Custody of the eyes" refers to the practice of deliberately turning your gaze away from things that are not meant for your sight or that might, by being seen, lead you into sin.

If it accidentally produces cockle among the wheat, there is no reason why the crop should be abandoned.[85]

The danger among interior souls of judging a course of action simply by possible motives and possible eventualities is a real one. If the action is believed to be pleasing to God, it should be confidently embarked upon; the outcome must be left to Him. Otherwise nothing will ever be done, and spirituality will become sterile. The gap between the holy diffidence of humility and the narrow unenterprise of laziness is small.

It is in the interest of the Devil to present the relative harm so as to cramp the soul's pursuit of the absolute good. This is illustrated in the experience of St. Bernard[86] when tempted, for reasons of humility, to come down from the pulpit on the occasion of his preaching a sermon that was clearly moving his hearers profoundly. "You came up into the pulpit to please me," said the voice of Christ in his soul, "and must you now go down from it to please the Devil?"

A third obstacle to the practice of penance voluntarily undertaken is the very natural fear people feel that, having once begun, they will have to mortify every appetite of every gratification all the time. Probably it is this factor — the dread that God may take advantage of their goodwill and make life dreary and empty for them — that deters souls more than any other. Souls are ready to respond to the invitation "Learn of me, because I am meek and humble of heart,"[87] but they do not want to respond to it so much that they will eventually have to

---

[85] Matt. 13:24-30.

[86] St. Bernard (1090-1153), Abbot of Clairvaux.

[87] Matt. 11:28.

say with St. Paul that they know Christ only as Christ crucified, and that with Him they are nailed to the Cross.[88] That
would be too much. And so they do nothing.

Just as there are men and women in the world who feel the
desire to enter religion but who are afraid of the consequences
of their vocation, so there are men and women in the world, as
well as in religion, who, although powerfully drawn to penance, shrink from its implications.

To value penance in the abstract, to be conscious of the
personal need for it, to see it as a positive act of love and not
merely as a restrictive exercise, and then not to perform it is a
neglect of grace. There is no blame to the man whose mind is
never crossed by the thought of penance; he will be required
to give a different account. But the man who knows the summons and yet fails it is blameworthy. Also he will not be happy
until he follows it.

The man who fasts and gives up his luxuries is not con-
demning himself to a life of boredom and frustration; he is
freeing himself of much that would otherwise tie him down.
By renouncing the amusements of the world, a man enlarges
his capacity for enjoyment. Just as unhappiness does not come
from the lack of material things but from the superfluity of material things, so happiness is not threatened by self-denial so
much as by self-indulgence.

Happiness and sanctity are not the same thing, but they
very often go together. Sanctity and voluntary mortification
are not the same thing, but it is difficult to see how they can
exist apart.

[88] Cf. 1 Cor. 2:2; Gal. 2:19.

"What can be more efficacious than fasting?" asks St. Leo in his thirteenth sermon. "By its observance, we are able to draw near to God, resist the Devil, rise above the persuasions of evil. From the practice of abstinence arise pure ideas, reasoned desires, right-minded counsels. By means of voluntarily imposed hardships, the desires of the body are restrained and the virtues of the spirit renewed."

∞

Penance has value only if it is united to Christ's Passion

If a member of the body wants to resemble the Head, he should want at the same time to blot out the debt incurred by sin. Penance satisfies both these desires. That Christ has atoned "once and for all"[89] does not rule out participation in Christ's atonement, does not mean that at this late stage there is nothing we can do. On the contrary, since the finite members live in a body that is infinite and eternal, there is everything we can do. We can unite our own finite penance to His, which is of infinite worth. Indeed it is only by doing so that our penances can assume the slightest value.

Although the Passion was a succession of vicarious acts of penance that took place in time, its significance belongs to eternity. It is by what we bring in the way of compassion, co-penance, and co-sacrifice that we show our willingness to be identified with His work. Since His sacrifice was voluntary, so should ours be. Once freely consenting to His purpose and His demand, we draw to our insignificant expressions of penance

[89] Cf. Heb. 7:27.

the force of His infinite merit; mystically we find our place in Christ's act of atonement.

Our fasting is nothing, our disciplines are nothing, but caught up into the mystery of Christ's sufferings, our halting movements, childish gestures of sympathy, become efficacious. They are worked in Him and by Him and with Him. To deny Him these childish gestures of sympathy, therefore, is to deny Him a medium through which His redemptive grace to the world continues to seek expression and might otherwise find greater scope.

So it is that St. Athanasius[90] can say, "If people come to you and tell you seldom to fast in case you should endanger your health, do not believe them or listen to them; it is the enemy who is suggesting these things through them. For when the disciples wanted to know how unclean spirits might be expelled, the Lord replied that only by prayer and fasting could this kind of devil be cast out."[91] The Fathers of the Church, evidently, did not shrink from the idea of voluntary corporal penance. They knew that the call of worldly prudence that urged a greater caution was all too often the call to come down from the Cross altogether.[92]

---

[90] St. Athanasius (c. 296-373), Bishop of Alexandria.
[91] Mark 9:27-28 (RSV = Mark 9:28-29).
[92] Cf. Matt. 27:40; Mark 15:32.

∾

Chapter Ten

Allow God to purify your soul

Granted that a man's sanctity is measured by his conformity to Christ, it follows that the closer I resemble my model, the more will I be called upon to suffer. Not only will the amount of suffering depend upon my fidelity to the likeness of Christ, but so also will the nature of the suffering. The outward features may bear little resemblance to the Passion; it is in the inward features that there is likely to be a parallel.

If the explanation of Christ's life is given in terms of suffering — "Ought not Christ to have suffered, and so to have entered into His glory?"[93] — then the lives of His disciples will reveal the same sign. But it does not follow that the sign will be revealed to the disciples who are suffering it. The sign of the cross is at the same time the sign of discipleship and sanctity. But because there can be satisfaction in the sense of crossbearing, the sign is often hidden from those most immediately involved.

The outward sign is a symbol; it is the inward reality, and the soul's response to the inward reality, that makes for the likeness to Christ.

[93] Luke 24:26.

Just as Christ's suffering was that of love rejected — "not this man, but Barabbas"[94] — before it was that of outward physical pain, so the disciple's suffering will in its essence consist in that which will call for the greatest act of faith if he is to relate it to the Cross of Christ.

To reflect the Passion in his own life, a man must be ready to forego the satisfaction of seeing how he can possibly be reflecting the Passion of Christ's life. A man's passion will not consist in being scourged and crowned with thorns and nailed to the Cross; it is far more likely to consist in sharing with Christ the dereliction of Gethsemane.[95]

The trial of faith and hope is more searching than the trial of bodily endurance, and in the nature of the case, the substance of the trial is that it is not appreciated as such. Just as in the physical order, the will sometimes has to drive the body to go on beyond the potential breaking point, so in the spiritual order, the will must insist on the service of love when to all appearances there is nothing left of love itself.

Authorities are inclined to speak of interior trials as if they were confined to attacks upon the virtue of faith, upon the soul's beliefs. In a sense, this is true: all our problems would be solved if we fully trusted God's word. Certainly the faith we hear about from preachers and writers must be understood to include confidence in God's handling of our souls and not merely be restricted to assent to revealed truth.

The kind of faith that is the mystic's specific act, which is indeed the stuff of his service, is that which surrenders blindly

---

[94] John 18:40.
[95] Matt. 26:36-45; Mark 14:32-41; Luke 22:39-46.

to God's wisdom in all its possible manifestations. This kind of faith assumes love and hope and unquestioning obedience.

∞

Through your suffering, God purifies your soul

It is a commonplace to observe that, in the Providence of God, the Cross is exactly fitted to the need and capacity of each individual soul. This being so, the spiritual man will not only receive the Cross in the spirit, as we have just seen, but he will receive it in connections that, just because they are spiritual, touch him closest.

Just as water finds its own level, so does the Cross. And the level of the Cross is always that at which it can do the soul the most good. The things that the soul holds most precious are those that bear the greatest share of the Cross. For instance, the man to whom the love of souls is a vital force in his life will experience agonies of anxieties regarding their salvation. The corruption of the innocent will be to him a nightmare; his soul will be harassed by the thought of unrepentant deaths. He will see how powerless he is to prevent the world from winning souls to itself; he will know the anguish of rejected love and ingratitude and misunderstanding. He will long to take the temptations of others, and even the guilt itself, upon himself. And all the time, he will be denied the knowledge that either his suffering or his offering is being of the least use to those he most wants to help.

Under the weight of such a cross as this — and again, it must be insisted that the soul sees it more as a weakness than as a cross — the only alternative to despair is trust in God. The soul may imagine that lunacy or suicide will probably be the outcome, but in the Providence of God, union with Him is the eventual outcome. The whole purpose of such a cross has been to lead the soul to the point of surrender, to the final acknowledgment of God's comprehensive love. The soul is being taught to say, "Christ loves souls even more than I do; He must be trusted to look after His own. Christ shrinks from sin even more than I do; He must be helped by my compassion in the endurance of its effects."

For years the soul may have to struggle in this most poignant of human sufferings, but once risen above the too-human element — that personal interest in the work for souls that seeks to mold others, and that sees in individual influence the sole means of bringing them to salvation — the love that is expended in the labor for mankind is surprisingly purified. From now on, the affairs of men, their temptations and their failures, are seen through the eyes of Christ.

Since, again, it is in the nature of the spiritual vocation to search for outward as well as inward equilibrium, the man of prayer is likely, even more than most men, to feel that he has missed his vocation and that he is in the wrong place. The stability in God's service, to which he feels he has a right, eludes him completely. He finds himself forever unsettled, a misfit in every environment, the victim of his own muddled approach long ago. What such a man has to believe — and this is the test of his faith on the particular issue — is that it is better to be in the wrong place by the will of God than in the right one by his own will.

The pain of this vocational trial lies in the conviction, mistaken but no less real on that account, that every circumstance arising out of life is in conflict with the soul's spiritual ambition. It is as if the very scaffold-poles that are meant for the building of the house are in fact being used as fuel to burn it down.

But such is precisely the value of the trial; it is to the extreme edge of faith that the soul has to be pushed. "The life of faith," says Caussade,[96] "is nothing else than a perpetual pursuit of God through everything that disguises, disfigures, destroys, and, if we may use the word, annihilates Him." The case cannot be expressed more strongly than that. In a world of apparent lunacy and false purpose, the soul has to cling to the assurance that Christ has triumphed over material things, and that the only reality is serving Him in spirit and in truth.[97]

A third example of how the Holy Spirit singles out the interior man for the most purifying of the trials to which souls must be subject if they are to make any progress is to be seen in the operation known as the dark night of the spirit. Here, in the region of the contemplative soul's most specific act — namely, the act of contemplation itself — is experienced not the closeness of the divine presence, but its absence. Where the whole desire of the soul stretches out in a single longing for God, there is nothing but desolation.

Loneliness is bad enough when a man is conscious of being cut off from his fellowmen, but when he feels cut off from God, there is nothing left. It is now that he has to hope where there are no grounds for hope, that he has to believe where the last shreds of faith seem to have worn away. "My God, my God,

---

[96] Jean-Pierre de Caussade (1675-1751), ascetic writer and author of the spiritual classic *Abandonment to Divine Providence*.

[97] John 4:23, 24.

why hast Thou forsaken me?"[98] is his cry. So he has good precedent for his prayer.

The more the soul searches in the darkness for God, the more clearly does it see the corruption of its own heart. If only its low motives, its insatiable greed, its past record of sin, and the evidence of its present selfishness could be swept out of the way, there might be some chance of drawing nearer to the lost presence of God. But there is always this mountain in between.

What the soul does not realize, because God is keeping back the knowledge, is that God is making the crooked ways straight. In the process of straightening, the ways look all the more crooked.

A base metal, thrown into the furnace, looks more base than ever before. The secret fires of charity make the base metal of self-love look base indeed. It is only as the field of wheat is growing to harvest that cockle is seen for what it really is. Until then the bad seed has been either underground or else pretty much resembling the good.[99]

∞

Christ suffers in, with, and through you

It will be noticed that each of the three trials outlined above — which, incidentally, are not normally experienced at the same time, but in the order corresponding to the rest of the soul's spiritual development — represents a purification of an interior faculty. From human anxiety and attachment to work among souls, which made up the substance of the first agony,

[98] Matt. 27:46; Mark 15:34.
[99] Cf. Matt. 13:25-30.

until the naked dependence upon God is reached in the third, the soul is being progressively cleansed as regards imagination, intellect, and will.

All the way through, moreover, there is this constant shadowing of the Agony in the Garden. How, when we come to think of it, could the sufferings of the mystic take any other form? It is through suffering that he plunges into the heart of Christ. Fear for the souls of men, noncomprehension of the earthly shape life has taken, estrangement from God and fellowmen: these make up the likeness that no other sufferings of human devising could bring about. This is Gethsemane.

The spiritual man does not have to rationalize his pain, finding arguments with which to convince his mind of its salutary effects; he can interpret it simply in terms of the Passion. The Christian does not have to order his mind like a Spartan; all he has to do is open his eyes like a mystic. The Passion is there for him to see. It is all around him; it is going on inside him. He fails as a Christian, let alone as a man of prayer, if he knows no more about it than what he learns from the printed page of history.

To leave suffering out of our conception of charity and religion is to leave out not only the antiseptic that keeps us strong in the service of God, but also the Passion from the Gospel itself. Christ has suffered not only in our midst as a historical figure, but also in our person as mystically identified.

Christ has taken our sorrows upon Himself, becoming pain not only *for our sake*, but *in us*. It is not only that we benefit by His sufferings, applying His pains to ourselves, but that He suffers in our sufferings, taking our pains to Himself. A deepening sense of this co-suffering in Christ is one of the graces of mysticism; it is an essential aspect of the mystic's advance. Having the evidence of the Passion before him, and knowing its implications, a man can never reasonably wonder why he is called upon to endure suffering. Physical pain, doubt, loneliness, fear, temptation: they are all there in Christ, and Christ is wholly here in me when I am suffering them.

The experience of suffering, like that of love, reveals a man to himself. And now, in the light that prayer brings to his soul, the experience of personal suffering is found to explain Christ's life, as well as his own, to a man. He begins to see the meaning of Christ's purpose, and when he does that, the purpose of his own existence shows up to scale.

Once a person has grasped the significance of pain in the world — once, that is, he has seen suffering humanity as an extension of Christ in agony, and therefore as something sacramental — he is in a position to see deeper and deeper into God's plan. The fog begins to lift, and he can see the horizon. At last he sees the real shape of things, matching it exactly with the shape taken by Christ in the world.

Pain, to such a one, is not a sad and necessary discipline to which he must adjust himself if he wants to find any sort of peace on earth; it is an opportunity not to be missed; it is a most welcome means of increasing his likeness to Christ.

The spiritual man does not have to force his prayer along channels that point to the crucifix. His prayer takes him to Christ, whom he cannot but know as the Man of Sorrows.[100] He does not have to stir up a devotion to the Passion; the Passion is present to him with the presence of God. No new

---

[100] Isa. 53:3.

spiritual technique has to be devised for the recognition of God's will in the problem of pain; pain is now to him a revelation like any other. It is an inspiration, a force that propels rather than a weight that depresses.

Living His life in us, promising to bring us joy more abundant, offering us a peace that He alone can give and that is not subject to disturbance from the world, Christ takes the evil out of pain, death, hopelessness, and desolation.

"If any man thirst, let him come to me and drink."[101] If any man suffer, let him come to me, and I will carry his cross for him, suffering in him and with him and through him.

If I do not see Christ as performing this office, I do not see Him properly at all. Christian mysticism is nothing other than this: the reliving of Christ in souls, the continued unfolding of His will and purpose among men.

"I wandered aimlessly like a lost sheep," says St. Augustine in his *Soliloquies*, "seeking Thee in exterior things when all the while Thou didst inhabit my very being. I grew fatigued in looking all about me, while actually Thou didst reside within me, because I had a desire for Thee. I have walked through the cities and squares of the world searching for Thee, and I have not been able to find Thee, because I sought in vain outside myself for that which was within my soul."

∞

You have a role in Christ's Passion

To summarize the doctrine: my approach to the whole question of suffering, whether presented as my own personal

[101] John 7:37.

problem or as the wider one of the suffering that is seen in the world, is not that of disguising an evil so that it looks like a good. It is to take up suffering as Christ's.

To superimpose an ideal, however laudable the intention, is to create an artificial relationship between what I shrink from and what I know to be sanctifying. Far more real is the relationship between suffering, which is in itself an evil, and Christ, who, in virtue of His taking it upon Himself, presents it to His Father as a good.

It would be idle to train a searchlight on a rubbish heap in the hopes that the insects would be dazzled into inactivity and that the general effect would be less unpleasant. More satisfactory would be to start a fire within. To approach pain from the outside is, at its most successful, to anaesthetize. More satisfactory is to get inside it and suffer it with Christ. The Christian must try to learn pain with the mind of Christ suffering.

What we find hard to realize, but what is nevertheless true, is the mutual incorporation of suffering in Christ — He so reproducing Himself in us that our sufferings become reproductions of His, and we, correspondingly, reproducing Him.

Pain, in the mystical life, is the practical and actual appropriation on our part of Christ's Passion, and, on His part, the assimilation into Himself of ours. So far as we are concerned, then, the sanctification of our crosses does not consist in bringing anything new to the sum of the Mystical Body's[102] pain and act of expiation; our contribution consists in uniting what is already there in us to what is already there in Christ.

---

[102] The Mystical Body of Christ is another name for the Church; cf. 1 Cor. 12:27.

By acknowledging as Christ's the trials that seem peculiarly our own, we are bearing witness to the Passion as effectively as though we had been present at it.

We are always preoccupied by the thought of what *else* we are to do if we are to sympathize actively with the sufferings of Christ. But it is not primarily a question of offering *more* compassionate sufferings; rather, it is a question of offering the existing sufferings with more compassion. This applies to both voluntary and inescapable suffering.

Wherever it is seen, pain is for the saint the continuation of Christ's Passion. For him the Gospel is forever expanding, taking new shape, finding fresh application, covering every event in the sequence of history. And always it is the same Word, the same Passion, the same Christ.

The *Agnus Dei* ("Lamb of God") of the book of Revelation is still standing as if it were slain.[103] The Yahweh of the Old Testament who, speaking through the prophet Isaiah, says, "I am still the same; before all and at the end of all, I am"[104] is the Father who reveals Himself in the New Testament in the Person of the Son. Everywhere and always it is the Lord. "Before Abraham was, I am."[105] To the saint, to the mystic, there is no contradiction in living thus with the Passion of Christ and outside the ordinary dimensions of time.

[103] Rev. 5:6.
[104] Cf. Isa. 43:10, 13.
[105] John 8:58.

Chapter Eleven

Be attentive to God in your soul

From what has been said, it follows that one of the first signs of the mystical life is the realization of God's presence working within the soul. Not that the abiding companionship is felt as such, but that the reality of the mystical indwelling is appreciated in a new way. Where before it was a doctrine to be acknowledged, now it is known to be a force. Indeed, it becomes the driving impulse of the soul's whole life. Where hitherto the passage from the first letter of St. John that teaches that "he who remains in charity abides in God and God in him"[106] has been understood in a general way, now, with initiation into mystical prayer, the text is seen to be a literal statement of fact. The idea of mutual indwelling is raised from the level of devotion to that of guiding principle. Instead of remembering it at intervals, particularly during thanksgiving after Holy Communion, the soul finds itself constantly referring to it and counting on it.

The discovery of God present in the soul is one of the most momentous in the soul's spiritual career. It gives quite a new conception to the soul's relationship with Christ — indeed,

---

[106] Cf. 1 John 4:16.

with the Blessed Trinity. And here the word *new* does not mean "novel"; the theology of it is beyond question.

The work of Christian perfection is understood to be not so much a process of copying the life of Christ, as an artist might stand back from his model and draw what he sees, line by line, but rather an adaptation of self to the life of Christ which is an unceasing activity within. Theologians, following the Fathers, are not afraid to call this mystical process — which at the same time is only the work of Christian perfection — by the name of deification. "Participation in the Holy Spirit is a participation in the divine nature," says St. Athanasius, "and if He descended upon men it was to deify them." This is assumed by St. Gregory Nazianzen[107] when he says, "If He is to have the power to deify us, He must Himself be God."

When we read in St. Paul that we are living temples of God, we are not being treated to a literary fancy, a phrase which is to be taken figuratively. It is more than a picturesque image; it is a positive theological fact. Commenting on the passage in Corinthians: "Do you not understand that you are God's temple, and that God's Spirit has His dwelling in you,"[108] St. Thomas says that "only the indwelling of God makes a soul the temple of God."

Once the soul has grasped the significance of this doctrine, the whole horizon changes; the implications are limitless; the service of God can never look quite the same again; the whole business of religion takes on a new color. Whether as the result of a sudden illumination or by means of a gradual dawning of

[107] St. Gregory Nazianzen (329-389), Bishop and Doctor.
[108] Cf. 1 Cor. 3:16.

knowledge, the mystical understanding of this truth is felt to be overwhelming and all-embracing. Everywhere the soul catches echoes of the Word, which is communicating itself within.

How does all this come about? Not, certainly, because of some fortunate trick of the imagination, a twist given to the direction of our thought. For Christ to become the life of our life, which is what this mystical view of existence amounts to, we need the light of grace. Without this light, Christ will never be more to us than an external pattern to be imitated, a voice to be listened for and obeyed.

But to souls who hunger and thirst for justice, who want nothing else but to follow up the gifts of the Holy Spirit and so to love God in full perfection, the light is not likely to be withheld. Of this much, anyway, we can be sure: those who correspond with the indwelling of the Holy Spirit, and who try to find the principle of their Christ-life from the life of Christ Himself within their souls, will discover that their prayer and their thought are increasingly being directed by a movement that they recognize as not their own.

More and more, the soul of prayer should come to realize that it is the Holy Spirit who is acting. More and more, the activity is understood to be taking place in the soul, and that the soul itself is waiting on the word of God. There is a difference between sensing something from without — as it might be the action of grace conveyed by the sight of a miracle — and knowing something from within. It is now the action of grace not so much *upon*, as *in*, the soul.

The life of the soul in grace resembles the life of the body in nature; each goes on all the time so long as there is not death.

The life communicated to the soul by the indwelling of the Holy Spirit is not spasmodic — any more than the life enjoyed by the body in the order of nature is subject to interruptions — and is moreover progressively sanctifying.

The Third Person of the Blessed Trinity interiorly effects our sanctification, is the source and cause of our sanctification — *is* our sanctification. Our sanctification is not brought about by Him as by a person walking at our side and encouraging us along the way until we finally reach the goal. It is brought about by the act of a Person imparting Himself to us within ourselves, and to whom we give our unqualified consent.

The grace of the Holy Spirit is not an exterior influence; it is a power developing in the nature of the soul. If we look for a human analogy, its operation is more like that of a talent or a habit. The Holy Spirit works in us in much the same way as we work in what we write, in what we say, or in what we teach. The Spirit of God is expressed in the spirit and in the lives of His servants.

But the analogy must not be pressed too far, for whereas man is the temporary agent of the labor he produces — he leaves his work when he has finished it — the Holy Spirit is the constant impulse of the work produced. If the Holy Spirit ceased to breathe within our souls, our love of God would cease. The Holy Spirit *is* our love of God.

There is no spirituality but that which is the work of grace, and the whole function of grace is to effect the transformation of the soul in Christ. All the time, the Holy Spirit labors in the soul so that Christ may be more perfectly reproduced.

St. Paul, uniting himself with the work of the Holy Spirit, says that he is in labor with the Galatians until Christ be formed in them.[109] This is the whole work, the whole problem. Once this has been achieved, Paul can go his way. But inside the souls of those Galatians, the Holy Spirit still, in the single act of indwelling, imparts and evokes the love of the Father.

"Until Christ be formed in you": the words hold out a promise. The assumption is that man is at least capable of taking Christ's form, of being transfigured by grace. Paul labors, the inspired word of revelation labors, and the indwelling Spirit Himself labors. How can man resist? How can Christ not be formed in man? How can man not be formed in Christ?

If God Himself looks for the formation of His Son in me, I have hope that His Spirit will achieve it. What He wants is not me but the image of Christ which I am designed to be. I carry this likeness not as something grafted on, but as something grown into from the depths of my being.[110] If my whole sanctity is Christ, how can it be something alien to me? It should be the most natural thing in the world. The most natural thing in the world is love, and God is love.

In fact, far from there being anything foreign to the nature of the soul in finding both its identity and its sanctity in this inward communication, the whole idea of self-realization in Christ supposes, in the meaning of the term, the realization of our natural as well as our supernatural qualities. As Christ's divine nature elevates and "deifies" us, so His human nature brings out in us the best that our natural characters are capable of producing.

[109] Gal. 4:19.
[110] Cf. Rom. 11:24.

Moreover, in any attempt on the part of man to return to the innocence lost by sin — let alone in any attempt to advance toward union with the exemplar Christ — the human side of man is not losing itself in an artificial or academic maze, but rather, is finding itself at a level of reality not prejudiced by the sin and superficiality of the world.

If Christ were the prototype alone, and not the very life itself of the Christian, there might be reason to wonder at the means adopted by different schools of spirituality or by different individuals in the work of imitating Christ. But because He lives His life through us, and because we live our lives in Him, the question as to how far the life of mystical identification can be genuine does not arise. It is an absolute fact, and that is all there is about it.

It may be held, then, with complete conviction that the baptized Christian who seeks to love God is seeking and loving because of Love Himself, who is really and not figuratively dwelling within his soul. It may be held further that unless sin intervenes and kills the life of grace in the soul, the fruits of this indwelling increase with the soul's spiritual maturity. Nothing is static in the spiritual life.

∞

Your sanctification
requires effort on your part

Although it would be true to say that the presence of the Holy Spirit in the soul is that which makes possible and actual the soul's sanctification — is itself the process of sanctification — it would be a mistake to imagine that the soul had nothing more to do than sit back and nod consent. To have appropriated the life and merits of Christ is not to have found a magic formula that relieves the individual from further responsibility. On the contrary, precisely because the soul has taken on the life of Christ, it has taken on the work of Christ and the sufferings of Christ. The idea of mutual indwelling connotes communion at every level: the whole of Christ is imparted to the whole of man; the whole of man is at the disposal of the whole of Christ.

If the Word is all the time seeking to express its own meaning through the personality of the individual man, then the individual man must be attuned to the mode of revelation. In His life on earth, Christ revealed Himself as a fellow laborer and fellow sufferer. In His life in the soul, He reveals Himself in the same terms. And in those terms, just as He did during His lifetime, He appeals for cooperation. Certainly the soul's awakening to the grace of divine indwelling is not the signal for taking a rest.

If there had been quietist implications in the doctrine, the Church would not have set Her seal upon its conclusions. Just as apathy is alien to physical health and development, so a supine reliance upon the indwelling of the Blessed Trinity irrespective of personal effort would be alien to spiritual health and development. It would be not only alien; it would be incompatible.

So if the Spirit of God is to bear fruit in the soul, the individual, on his part, must be ready to tread the ordinary road of Christian perfection. There is no getting out of the common discipline. A man must go on being good, even though Christ inside him is achieving his perfection for him — all the more reason.

The Thessalonians were told by St. Paul not to extinguish the Spirit.[111] To the Ephesians he wrote, "Grieve not the Holy Spirit of God, whereby you are sealed unto the day of redemption."[112] By the neglect that either amounts to sin or leads to it, we can extinguish the fire of the Spirit and grieve the indwelling Spirit of God.

∞

Attention to God will transform you

In what way, it might be asked, does the doctrine of the indwelling affect a person's life? Granted that it is a fact, how does it influence the interior and exterior conduct of the soul? In the actual exercise of prayer, does the person praying know that anything specific is taking place, and in relation to life as a whole, is there any difference of outlook?

As regards prayer, the difference made by this perception of the Christ-life present and operating within the soul is that the work of the imagination virtually ceases. While the higher faculties are attending, with greater or lesser actual and formulated deliberation, to the indwelling, the lower faculties, not interested in this grace except devotionally, are at a loss and must find their outlets not during the time of interior prayer at all, but in more extroverted exercises.

The divine indwelling, partly because its work in the soul is deep and silent, and partly because the essential element cannot be easily pictured in the mind, is a grace that relates to faith far more than to feeling. Consequently, it is in the prayer

[111] 1 Thess. 5:19.
[112] Eph. 4:30.

of faith, rather than in discursive prayer, that this presence of God is contemplated.

Attention to God within the soul assumes so much and argues about so little that, apart from whatever methods may be necessary to recollect the soul at the beginning or to get rid of conscious distraction, set forms of prayer are almost entirely dispensed with. Accordingly, the prayer tends to become very simple, less dependent than before upon self-expression. Images, incentives, and speculations are not so much cut down by an act of the will as instinctively discarded. It is a reversal of what it was before: considerations that previously proved helpful are now found to be distracting; the silence that previously got on one's nerves is now felt to bring peace.

The same quiet attention to the indwelling presence of God — or in any event, the same quiet desire to attend to it — is experienced by monks when reciting the Divine Office. Indeed, the difference between vocal and mental prayer is felt to be slight; since the exercise common to both is now simply waiting interiorly upon God, it hardly seems to matter whether this is being done to the accompaniment of words or against a background of silence.

As in the case of prayer, so in the wider approach, any idea that the appropriation of Christ's merits may allow for a slackening of effort is out of the question. The indwelling, far from justifying inactivity, in practice seems to inspire works of charity. And this is not to be wondered at when the individual can confidently believe that it is Christ within him who is working through his agency.

Works that in the beginning of the spiritual life were undertaken with mixed feelings of doubt, desire, dread, and hope for the best are now accepted in a spirit of trust. Knowing that it is as much in his work as in his suffering that the disciple must resemble his Lord, the individual looks straight at Christ and hardly at all at self.

It is recorded that St. Catherine of Siena[113] was told by our Lord: "I never cease to make you like unto myself. . . . I desire to renew in your soul that which happened in my life." The indwelling in the soul is not the dead Christ in the tomb; it pursues the course of "that which happened in my life."

It follows that as this intuitive perception of Christ dwelling within the soul deepens and becomes, under the influence of infused grace, habitual, a new mode of knowledge is acquired. A wisdom is learned that handles the natural in a supernatural way, and which takes the supernatural for granted. This is called mysticism.

But it is not to be thought on this account that the supernatural mode of knowledge necessarily satisfies the mind. On the contrary, it may very well, and normally does, give pain to the mind. Just *because* its apprehensions are spiritual, the new knowledge is painful to the intellect. The human and material are at home among things human and material. When the familiar things have to be interpreted according to a law that is unfamiliar, the law of the spirit, there is no sense of security in the consciousness. It is this want of sureness that calls for the act of faith. This is the whole point.

The indwelling of the Three Persons of the Blessed Trinity in the soul does not supply for the act of faith. In this life, there is no substitute for either faith, hope, or love. The indwelling

[113] St. Catherine of Siena (c. 1347-1380), Dominican tertiary.

does not take the place of the theological virtues; it develops them.

Under one or another aspect — whether of faith, hope, or charity — the virtue or knowledge that is born of the graces we have been considering becomes the driving power of the soul's action. It is a perception of reality, although the soul may not recognize it as such. The soul is stretching out toward truth. And the light of truth can be blinding to the eyes.

In a simple and intuitive act, the soul reduces its concepts of truth and reality and life to the single idea of God. God is the All. The way and the truth and the life are one. It is only supernatural knowledge that can give this vision. And when possessed of this vision, the soul finds that it is blind. We are back again to faith. The mystical life is the life at once of faith and of vision, of darkness at one level and light at another.

Although this primary conception of all being resolves itself into the bare thought of God, it is not so much an exclusive as a comprehensive act. It is not that the soul sees nothing else but God — because, as we shall note later on, the soul's vision of God is painfully darkened — but that everything is seen in relation to the supernatural rather than to the natural.

The mind begins to form its judgments according to the one supernatural criterion, begins to look in people for one kind of response, and begins to estimate results by one standard only. The scene is found to have changed; the supernatural is found to be taking first place.

The knowledge resulting from this new view of truth is something that unaided reason could not arrive at. Reason can assent to the truth, can approve of the new knowledge that apprehends the truth so easily and which the truth in its turn enlarges, but it cannot of itself arrive at either the knowledge or the truth. This particular wisdom is arrived at by intuition and personal experience — in other words, by infused grace.

Reason can follow St. Thomas and see that God is present in His creatures by essence, presence, and power, but unless reason has been interiorly informed of the indwelling as a personal reality, the knowledge is just another piece of information. St. Thomas argues that God inheres in every created work as the cause of its being and in every activity as the source of its operation. This may well be the means whereby infused knowledge is conveyed to the soul. But it is not the cause of this knowledge. The cause is the divine light.

"In Thy light we shall see light"[114] — not in any creature's light, but in the Holy Spirit's light. That which teaches is Divine Wisdom; that which is received is faith. All supernatural faith is the free gift of God, and what we are considering here is the supernatural gift of theological faith further illumined by grace. The light that shines here is the kind that normally brings darkness to the mind. It is the darkness on which Dionysius and St. John of the Cross particularly are the authorities, and it is one into which the contemplative soul must be introduced.

The purpose of darkness is to provide the setting for the birth of mystical knowledge and contemplative prayer. And *setting* means more than a suitable atmosphere: the darkness is itself an instrument, an agent. In the sense that it is a direct result of grace, it is itself a grace. As regards the dawn of the

[114] Ps. 35:10 (RSV = Ps. 36:9).

mystical life, darkness is, paradoxically, the contributing factor of light. But of darkness more will be said in another place.

∞

You can come to know Christ
through His presence in your soul

"How long a time have I been with you, Philip, and you have not known me?"[115] Since our Baptism, the indwelling has been a fact in our lives, a fact that only mortal sin can repudiate, but to how many of us has it been a conscious reality? Have we grown in our apprehension of Christ within — have we "known" Him? It seems that, right up to the end, the Apostles, expecting the victorious Messiah, mistook the essential Christ.[116]

It is possible for us, like the Apostles, to get no further than the Miracle Worker, the Teacher, the Leader. As the Apostles got no nearer than what their senses told them of Christ, than what their affections responded to, so the tendency with us is also to stop on in the apprehensions of sense when all the time we should be searching in the spirit.

Until Christ left them so as to come to them at another level, He was not fully "known" by even His closest friends on earth. "It is expedient therefore that I go, for if I go not, the Paraclete will not come to you."[117] Now, with the indwelling of the Holy Spirit — His own Spirit — in the human soul, Christ is made known as He wishes to be made known.

[115] Cf. John 14:9.
[116] Acts 1:6.
[117] John 16:7.

But when we have said all that we can say about the grace of divine indwelling, we come back to what Revelation itself says about it. In the discourse following the analogy of the vine, and in speaking of the true vine, our Lord is preaching nothing else but the doctrine of mutual indwelling; we have the words of Christ's prayer to the Father: "The glory which Thou hast given me I have given them. . . . I in them and Thou in me, that they may be made perfect in one . . . that the love wherewith Thou hast loved me may be in them and I in them."[118]

"As many as received Him, He gave them power to be made the sons of God, to them that believe in His name, who are born, not of blood nor of the will of the flesh nor of man, but of God. And the Word was made flesh and dwelt among us . . . full of grace and truth."[119]

[118] John 17:22-23, 26.
[119] John 1:12-14

Chapter Twelve

Dwell in God

When St. Paul says that in God "we live and move and have our being,"[120] he must mean that by participation in the life of Christ and union with the Father and the Holy Spirit, we are, although human, transposed to a level of life and action and nature that is divine.

Man must forever remain other from God. The essence of God may never be communicated to the essence of man to the extent that man shares God's self-existent being. The being of man must remain distinct from the being of God, which is infinite and incommunicable and unique. But, on the showing of St. Paul, man can get very close to Him nevertheless.

In the foregoing chapter, we dwelt upon the truth that unfolds His life in us; in what follows, we shall see that it is equally true — and indeed, more theologically accurate — to say that we unfold our lives in Him. Where the relationship of the mutual indwelling is concerned, the dependence is man's, not God's. The life of the Blessed Trinity cannot require the life of a human being in which to dwell and express itself; the life of human beings, on the other hand, is conditioned by

[120] Acts 17:28.

the existence of the Blessed Trinity, in which man lives and moves and has his being.

God, then, does not take a shape from the soul in which He dwells; the responsive soul takes its shape from God. The potentiality that is at the beginning formless can become set in God. It is the whole business of religion, Christianity, and mysticism, so to set the human soul.

By Baptism, the soul enters in; by fidelity and cooperation, the soul lives ever more fully and moves ever more surely; by the grace of infused contemplation,[121] the life, movement, and being of man are taken over from sense to spirit. In the unitive way, the life is shared with the life of God, the movement is actuated by the will of God, and the being is deified by the nature of God.

"A certain nature may be ascribed to a certain thing in two ways," says St. Thomas. "First essentially; second by participation. Thus, after a fashion, man becomes a partaker of the divine nature." The spirituality a man practices is not a thing of his own; it is that element of God's love that is his because of his place in God. "These virtues," says St. Thomas in the same article and alluding to the theological virtues which are beyond the nature of man to practice, "are proportionate to man in respect of the [divine] nature of which he is made a partaker."

It is when the spirit of a man is informed by the Spirit of Christ that this living in God is accomplished. The man may not be able to point to a moment when the identification took

---

[121] "Infused contemplation" refers to prayer involving simple attention to God that springs from divine inspiration.

place, may not be able to explain the transformation that has been going on in him, and may not even know at first that anything very significant has happened to him; but a special kind of life in God has begun.

"In this we know that we abide in Him, and He in us: because He has given us of His Spirit."[122] Why, then, are not all aware of this? How is it that the Holy Spirit makes some so vividly conscious of the fact, and others not at all? The answer seems to be that where there is more charity, there is greater awareness, and that where the awareness is keenest, there is accompanying knowledge that the charity is the gift of God and not anything that one has oneself worked up.

God does not pledge Himself to live His life as fully and as recognizably in all souls alike. St. Augustine makes this point clear when he says, "God does not dwell in each and every creature to which He is present; and even in the very ones in whom He dwells, He does not dwell in all in the same measure." The saints are those in whom there is the least obstacle to the life of Christ within the soul, and to whom it is granted to enter most closely into the life of God. The life lived by the saints is the life more abundant, both the life and the abundance coming unmistakably from God.

The effect of this mystical perception of life in Christ is that the soul appreciates more and more the immanence of God and the weakness of human effort. God is known to be the Absolute, the All, and in relation to this fact, man is nothing. God's omnipotence is felt to be the force of every created activity, the significance of all sanctity, the cause and movement

[122] Cf. 1 John 3:24.

and end of love. With Isaiah, the soul can say, "Lord, Thou wilt give us peace, for Thou hast wrought all our works for us."[123] Whatever there is in us of virtue, of self-discipline, and of prayer is His work and recognized as His work. We have nothing to offer but what He has first given. He is all.

Another consequence of being able to see how the soul can be said to have life in Christ, and one that marks an advance on previous mystical perceptions, is the tendency to view created good in God instead of seeing God in created good. Of pleasure the soul does not have to say, "God's will is in this; I may accept it without scruple." In the enjoyment of beauty, the soul does not have to say, "God is hidden in what I see; He is revealing Himself to me through natural forms." When moved toward another in friendship, the soul does not have to say, "God disguises Himself in the appearance of this person; I must look for God in him and love only that part."

Instead of this, which is a frontal attack upon the outer wall of the problem, the soul sees, as if looking down upon the city of God from the air, what it is searching for. All things are within, and all things belong to Him whom they reveal and express.

The soul that, in the words of St. Leo, "is mindful of the dignity of having been made a participator of the divine nature" will find that there is no longer the same need as before to indulge in change, amusement, and recreation. The self-subsistent nature of God is imparting a new stability to the soul; the simplicity of God is awakening a single-mindedness in the soul.

[123] Isa. 26:12.

This is what you would expect as a result of a union between strength and weakness, between everything and nothing. Possessed of a life infinitely more perfect than natural life, the soul is translated into a kingdom where the justice and the love and the holiness of God are there for the asking. The treasures of virtue are inexhaustible.

"Transforming souls into Himself," says St. Cyril of Alexandria, "the Spirit of God imprints on them a divine image and traces in them the likeness of the supreme substance." And the same saint again: "The Holy Spirit calls us from nothingness into being. He restores the image of God when He impresses His lines in our souls and transforms them, so to speak, with His own proper quality."

In many places, St. Cyril comes back to this idea that the grace of deification means a cooperation of activity. "If the fragrance of spices transmits its strength to the clothing and transforms into itself, as it were, those things in which it resides, why cannot the Holy Spirit, since He naturally exists in God, make those things in whom He resides, participants of the divine nature?" As the clothing gives out the fragrance, so the soul gives out grace.

To those who are settled in the mystical habit, the practice of detachment is not so much an act of stripping self as one of ignoring self. The soul, occupied with God, is unoccupied with self. Possessing and possessed by God, the soul is dispossessed of self. Humility, trust, belief in human nature, hospitality and generosity — all these things are instinctively felt to be suitable, as well as virtuous, and are practiced quite simply for the love of God. It is the love of God that simplifies and purifies their practice.

Where self had previously asserted claims on perfection, it now stands back and lets God work His own perfection as He wills. The more he is kept out of the picture, the better the individual is pleased. He knows that nothing is to be gained by having a stereotyped holiness in mind and fighting for it. Where laziness and discouragement say, "What's the use?" and settle down to do nothing, the confidence born of life in Christ says, "He will manage things if He wills to" and perseveres with the work in a spirit of complete indifference as to the material outcome.

To know in an experimental way that one's life is "hidden with Christ in God"[124] leaves little room for vanity, greed, fear, envy, and humbug. With Him we are buried to the old life, and with Him we are raised to the new.[125] Whether we live or die, whether we are present or absent, whether we are in darkness or in light, in suffering or in joy, we are the Lord's[126] and our lives are lived by Him and in Him.

∞

Union with God enables you to be truly you

Even while taking the doctrine, and taking it almost verbally from the Fathers and Doctors of the Church, we must guard against a Parsee, Buddhist, or Neoplatonist[127] conception

---

[124] Col. 3:3.

[125] Cf. Rom. 6:4.

[126] Cf. Rom. 14:8.

[127] Parseeism is a modified form of Zoroastrianism, which teaches that there is a continuous struggle of the universal spirit of good with the spirit of evil. Buddhism teaches that the soul, through self-denial and right thinking, can reach a divine

of this incorporation into God. Whereas a non-Christian theology would make the soul merge into the Divinity to the elimination of the individual, the mystical theology of the Church insists on the continuing identity of the person.

The soul loses nothing of that which was separately created by God; the individuality of each single soul as it exists in the mind of God remains distinct. The absorption does not obliterate; it enriches and re-creates. In human relationships, it is possible for the dominant personality to flatten out the other until there is virtually nothing of the original character left. In the relationship with God, where the soul is lost in the divine nature, the case is entirely different: the original character is found. The man's soul is more truly his own because it is united with, and realized in, God, than if it had followed nature and united itself with creatures.

Whether the soul knows it or not, its true happiness is an identification with the happiness of God. Its end is to find itself in God. When, consequently, the soul makes the happiness of God its own happiness, the holiness of God its own holiness, and the life of God its own life, there can be no diminution of either power or identity, but rather the reverse. I move by the grace of God, and by the grace of God I am what I am.[128] Because I move by the grace of God, I move all the faster. Because I am what I am by the grace of God, I am all the more myself.

> state of release from misdirected desire. Neoplatonism is a school of philosophy that recognizes a single source from which all existence emanates and with which the soul seeks mystical union.

[128] 1 Cor. 15:10.

Together with the soul's clarified view of its position in God must come, then, a clarified view of its own position as a reflection of God's image. And it is not just any reflection, but my reflection. God does not reflect Himself according to a universal image, but according to a particular interpretation. When we respond to Him with the complete surrender of ourselves, we are not putting ourselves on a shelf where we find a million other exact replicas of God.

By allowing ourselves to be fashioned by the Spirit who dwells within us, and in whom we dwell, we join a company of highly individual beings who serve a common purpose and have found a common good. Each with his own happiness shares the happiness of everyone else and the happiness of God. Until this pooling of natural and supernatural good is understood, charity is a piecemeal affair.

Charity comes into its own in the communion of saints. Joined in the love of God and of one another, recipients of God's love in whom they dwell, the saints of the Church on earth and in Heaven are those who best interpret the Gospel to the unbeliever. The saint is the Gospel ideal repersonified; he is a reverberation of the Word.

But in all this, it must be understood that the self that sets me apart from the self of another remains. In order to echo, I must give out a sound of my own; in order to be molded according to a model, I must have something to mold. What I must do is interpret, repersonify, within the limits of the medium at my command — namely, within my own personality.

The reason a facsimile can never be a work of art is because the essence of the thing copied is left out. The facsimile exactly reproduces the surface; it interprets nothing. For a true work of art, the essence of the thing represented has to be understood, seized upon, and, in harmony with the medium employed, conveyed.

Even in the surrender of my life to Christ, I cannot strictly *substitute* the being of Christ for the being that is myself. What I do is let His Spirit take the place of mine. If nothing of myself remained, there would be nothing more to give; the continuity of self-surrender would be broken.

When a man says to the girl he is to marry: "I give you my whole heart; henceforth it is all yours," he does not hand over a heart that thereafter is dead. He gives one that is thereafter all the more alive — but one that is directed and united.

∞

God's presence gives and sustains all life

Thus, it may be said that the raising of man's nature so that it partakes of the life and act of the Blessed Trinity is not only a vitalizing factor in the spirituality of the Christian; it is *the* vitalizing factor. This presence of God, whether considered as His life present in me or my life present in Him, is the source of life — is life itself. It is the whole doctrine of grace.

Viewed in its mystical context, this fact transcends all anthropomorphic connotations and is concerned with a very direct and simple apprehension. Indeed, as the soul's interior life develops, the doctrine is found to shed its more sensible associations, becoming increasingly both the principle and the meaning of activity, existence, and being.

God's presence, God's immanence, God's love: by it — not by *them*, but by it — the universe is supported, history is kept moving, and prophecy is fulfilled. By it — not by slogans *about* it, but by it — the individual soul finds peace. By it, sanctity is realized, eternal happiness is glimpsed, and the mystery of human existence is explained. Apart from it, nothing has any point. He is All.

Chapter Thirteen

Search for the light of God

All that has been considered in these pages hitherto has pointed to a more enlightened state of spiritual understanding. Such an understanding is not merely one that is better developed or better informed; it is one that is intuitive. Whether in the practical or strictly interior field — although especially in the interior field — it represents a judgment informed by infused grace.

Where natural understanding is eclipsed by supernatural understanding, you get one light obscured by another. You get darkness. As the light of a fire can hardly be seen in the light of the sun, and as the light of the stars is extinguished by the brightness of the moon, so the human intellect is darkened by spiritual enlightenment. Allowing it to be reasonable that a lower mode of knowledge should be put to confusion at the acquisition of a higher — even to the extent of requiring a state of unknowing — why, it might be asked, does the new and greater light bring darkness?

The answer is that the soul is accustomed to one form of light and cannot easily get used to another. The painter who works in a basement will have to adjust himself to the colors he sees in the open air. The light of day seems to take the color out of what he sees; he prefers the nearer and relatively brighter light of his neon bulbs downstairs. If he looks at the sun, he sees no light at all. The sun brings darkness to his eyes.

But say the artist steps out in the sunshine. After a while, he sees more in the colors that are everywhere around him than he has seen in the paints he has been using indoors. Knowledge, when the soul has become used to the action of grace, resumes its ordinary functions. The soul, illumined by the brighter light of mystical perception, judges clearly the problems presented to it in the lesser light of nature.

∽

Darkness prepares you to receive God's light

The above is by way of introduction and explanation. The theory must now be verified in terms of concrete experience. As typifying the experience of souls embarking upon the life of contemplative prayer, the case of the Apostles is representative. What the saints and mystics have contributed since the time of the Apostles is in the nature of confirmation rather than discovery.

Knowing Christ too humanly and obviously, as we have already seen, the Apostles were to have their knowledge raised to another plane. The translation from one level of apprehension to another was not only accompanied by, but occasioned by, darkness. The light was the cause, but the darkness was the occasion, of the change.

With our textbook ideas about spirituality, we tend to think of darkness as relating only to the act of prayer. But darkness is more than just aridity. The night is experienced, certainly, in the contemplative's specific activity; it is in prayer that the darkness primarily does its work. But it is a darkness that covers the whole earth.

We know nothing of the Apostles' prayer, but we know enough about their lives to see how they were subjected to the purifying discipline of darkness. Darkness is the heightening, under provocation, of the life of faith — "Blessed are they who have not seen but have believed"[129] — and this extends to every aspect of life.

When the lights go out in all the corridors that were thought to lead to God, and when the soul is left groping in what is feared to be the wrong direction, the intensification of faith is such that nothing but love and hope can support the strain that is put upon it.

Darkness is not only prayer going wrong; it is everything going wrong. And over and above this, it is having to believe that everything is going right.

Darkness is failure. The Apostles had to experience failure with Christ before they could experience triumph with Christ. They had to know, proof positive, their own weakness before they could know the strength that Christ was giving them — before they could know that the strength was Christ's and not their own. They must see themselves scattered, without hope, "scandalized this night in Him."[130] They must not only fail with Christ, but fail, apparently, without Him. They were to know the humiliation of not being ready at the moment when He supremely needed them. They were to watch their hopes die with Him — but from a safe distance. All this was darkness:

[129] John 20:29.
[130] Cf. Matt. 26:31.

the Apostles had to be cured of their false ideas about themselves and about Christ.

Darkness is fear, is regret, is doubt. Darkness is looking back and saying, "I have been deluded from the start; it has all been a mistake." Darkness is looking forward and saying, "I do not know what to do next; I have lost my way, and it is too late now to find it." It is the endlessness of darkness that constitutes its peculiar pain.

To the scattered Apostles who looked, from their safe distance, at the tomb, there was no light on the future whatever. And the light on the past had gone out. Nothing could be more final than a tomb, and with the abiding thought of that finality, their lives would somehow have to go on until they died.

Yet all the time this was light, light burning into their souls and not to be recognized as such until the work of purification had been brought about. The elements that seem to be destroying the possibility of life in Christ are those chosen to promote life in Christ. The enemies to our sanctification are precisely those that serve us best. Only the light that comes out of the darkness can teach us this.

Light is painful because "the darkness cannot comprehend the light":[131] the light is inexplicable. It is seen as contradictory. But in the end it is seen as sense.

Truth is not understood by falsehood. Yet truth demands to be understood. So falsehood has to be burned away in the dark fires of true light. Beyond a certain point, the soul cannot get rid of falsehood and imperfection. Darkness must come in to

[131] John 1:5.

do the work. Until falsehood and imperfection have given place to truth and perfection, they have to be endured painfully; they have to be seen for what they are. It is the light burning through the darkness that shows them up.

Darkness is not only when our ideals are shown to be unattainable, but also when they are shown to be not ideas at all — when they are seen to be selfish ambitions.

Darkness is not only when our motives are misunderstood and condemned, but also when they are seen by us to have been worthy of condemnation — when we realize that we ourselves have misunderstood them all along.

Darkness is not only when our zeal for souls is blocked at every turn, but also when we discover that it never has been zeal for souls. Darkness is seeing what zeal we have for self.

Only when we know that we have nothing of our own to show for our service of God, that we have no offering to make but our failures, sins, helplessness, and folly, are we made empty enough to be restocked with new graces. It is light through darkness that brings us to this stage. Now, at last, when humility has been learned by experience and not merely practiced as a duty, can a new order of perfection be established in the soul. The order of perfection is now not ours but God's. It is what He has wanted to bring all along, but what He has been prevented from establishing because He has not found us empty.

We thought we had surrendered self, but we had surrendered only the self that we saw and liked to surrender. It had to be in the darkness that we learned what our real selves were. The darkness was necessary to show us that our real selves had never been surrendered at all. Oh yes, we had done our best;

we had surrendered as much as we could. But God wanted more, and we were not ready to give it. And if God had not come with His darkness, we never would have been ready to give. So in the darkness, under cover of a night so black that we saw nothing of what was going on, God took.

Even our own self-surrender, then, is the gift of God. He makes it possible and actual; all we have to do is consent. The consent is so precious to Him that He wants it renewed again and again. It is in the night that our consent, touching the hundred different forms of disappointment and frustration, is constantly being repeated. Then, when the night has done its work, the consent is ratified by divine acceptance.

Superficially we do not feel that we are consenting — that is the whole point — but in the remote regions of the will, there is consent. If pressed, we would not dream of refusing. And it is the will that represents us. I am what my will is, and my will is what I am. I am not my emotions.

The contradictions of life, the inconsistencies and even incompatibilities, have to be assumed in the act of faith — or rather, in the habit of faith. They do not have to be accounted for or explained away; they have to be blindly endured. How else but in the darkness can this faith be brought to a finished perfection?

The essential vocation, the primary call to which our response is of supreme moment, is not to this or that exercise, but to love. This is the initial grace — love. To work out this grace on our own is beyond us. We need more grace. We need Love Himself to do it for us.

Love works in faith, and faith means the night. The lesson of our own insufficiency has to be forced in upon us by experience, by the revelation of self which is cruelly stark and shaming, by practical concrete evidence. Anyone can give a notional assent to the proposition: "I am a weak man"; what God wants is a more absolute recognition than that.

Nature seeks to live by feeling and by sight, but "the just man liveth by faith."[132] The ordinary familiar order of everyday has to be reversed. Instead of seeing what he wants to see and believing the rest, a man is forced to see what he does not want to see and has the utmost difficulty in believing anything.

One of the features of this darkness is the all-pervading sense of disillusion. It overrides confidence in human nature — let alone confidence in God — and leaves the soul hopelessly unsure of itself and in a state of defeat. The prevailing temptation is to bitterness, resentment, and despair. For as long as the Apostles had illusions about themselves and about their relationship with our Lord, they were not walking strictly in truth. They had to be disillusioned in order to be true. Their values were artificial; their conceptions were fanciful and unreal. It is the same with us. We have to be disillusioned.

Love cannot come to the soul except on its own terms. It does not mix with unreality and untruth. Love is the way and the truth and the life. Man must allow love to choose the way of darkness if this is the only way to truth and life. Just because faith is a life and not a single act of assent, the process of learning must go on for as long as there is life. Truth is inexhaustible. Light admits of deeper and deeper penetration.

Neither books nor directors nor penance nor systems of prayer can do service for the training that the Spirit Himself

[132] Hab. 2:4; Rom 1:17.

imparts. The soul must "be still and wait for the Lord."[133] Always there will be that pendulum swing of darkness and light, knowing and unknowing, learning and unlearning, losing and finding again. But obscurity on one plane means enlightenment on another. Loss and gain have to be judged according to a new standard, and there has been no waste. Not even the prayers and penances that, seen now in retrospect to have been so selfishly offered, are wasted. They were the best that could have been offered at the time.

When the soul has given back everything that belonged to God already, and when the soul knows that what is given is not its own, then is the time for spiritual possession. In the end, Christ comes not only to take away what He wants to take away — which is His in any case — but to occupy what He wants to occupy — which again is His.

---

[133] Cf. Ps. 36:7 (RSV = Ps. 37:7).

Chapter Fourteen

Imitate the harmony of Christ

In our search for perfection, we are inclined to equate the Christ-life with our own particular type of life; we see holiness in a mirror. If I admire austerity, I think of Christ as fasting for forty days and forty nights.[134] If my fancy is for the apostolic life, I think of Him primarily as so much given to preaching that He had not enough leisure even to eat.[135] And so on.

What this means in practice is that when I am being austere, I imagine myself to be holy; when I am laboring for souls, I see myself in the likeness of Christ. But in reality, it is not so much that I am making Christ a model for myself as that I am making myself a model for Christ.

The saint is the one who approaches his study of Christ with the open eye. He looks to Christ for a lead. He wants to see Christ as He is, and not as someone who must be fitted into a frame of perfection. For the saint, there is no frame of perfection. Perfection is Christ.

We do not have to look for perfection in Christ before we seek to be perfect according to His Spirit. We do not have to

[134] Matt. 4:2.
[135] Mark 3:20.

151

look for opportunities in life before we decide to follow them for the love of God. We do not have to plan our service of God before we start serving God. We do not have to wait for evidence of the lovable in people before we exercise charity.

In all these things, it works the other way around; we make directly for the essential good and the rest follows suit. "Seek ye first the kingdom of God."[136] "To them who love God, all things work together for good."[137] "Be ye perfect as your heavenly Father is perfect."[138] The emphasis is on the love of God, not on the realization of our dreams about the love of God.

"You have not chosen me, but I have chosen you."[139] If we had chosen Him, it might be different. As it is, we have to fit into the idea that He has of us, or we shall miss Him altogether — and miss ourselves.

To develop accidentals of sanctity at the sacrifice of sanctity is one of the most common of spiritual errors. In order to be holy, we have to match the holiness of our heavenly Father, we have to be identified with Christ, and we have to form one spirit with the Spirit of God. The whole of me must be fitted to God in union. There must be nothing left over, nothing independent, nothing eccentric or singular. The sanctity of Mary consisted precisely in the exact conformity of her soul with the will of God. "Be it done according to Thy word."[140] In Mary's soul there was the perfect balance of virtues. Every

---

[136] Matt. 6:33.
[137] Rom. 8:28.
[138] Matt. 5:48.
[139] John 15:16.
[140] Cf. Luke 1:38.

quality and power of her being was in the position that was designed for it.

The man who is imperfectly unified will find the greatest difficulty in becoming a saint. The man who is forever riding his own idea of sanctity may do much good as a propagandist, but he is unlikely to achieve true holiness. In the Providence of God, such a man may be raised up to correct a prevailing misconception, to found a religious order, or to catch the attention of a single soul in need. But it is hard to see how such a man is going to be selfless enough, flexible enough, to take the shape of Christ.

To be at one within ourselves, we need to reflect the mind of Christ, who prayed to the Father that "they may be one as we also are one, I in them and Thou in me."[141] When we have attained to this unity, there will be no longer any danger of exaggerating an aspect of sanctity to the detriment of love.

But until then, we can, like people standing in front of a convex or concave mirror at a fair, falsify the reflection. We can make a travesty of perfection, throwing out this or that characteristic from the pattern and turning the effect into a caricature. Asceticism, obedience, generosity, prayer: all can be used to turn against the one purpose they were designed to serve. The soul must always come back to the one way, truth, and life.

In the Person of Christ, we have not only the idea of human perfection as it exists in the mind of the Father made actual for our benefit; we also have God Himself. Possessing God Himself expressed in human form, we know both as much as

[141] John 17:22-23.

the human mind can know about God and, at the same time, what it is that God wants in the way of perfection out of us. In the measure that we conform to Christ, we shall be whole, balanced, true, and perfect.

For the meeting of the human personality with the divine, there must be a correspondence of terms. The harmony of parts that exists in its perfection in Christ must be met by a corresponding harmony, according to its degree, in the human soul. Where there is a deviation or exaggeration, there is an area that Christ does not cover. A lid cannot fit if there is a bulge in the side of the box. The likeness to Christ in the soul is never likely to come about so long as idiosyncrasy, fanaticism, a preoccupation with a devotional practice, or a mania for a particular doctrine can claim a place.

Some souls are by nature more balanced than others, and these start off at an advantage. For them, the operation of grace is a tranquil process — like the dew penetrating the fleece in Gideon's vision.[142] Others have to submit to being peeled of their natural rind like an orange. Others again must have their hard crust of temperament broken to bits before grace can get through — as though grace were acting on the shell of a nut.

But those to whom the transformation from nature to grace does no violence are not exempt from the night. It merely means that for them, the dark knowledge of God is distributed more evenly over the cognitive faculties of the soul. Whereas the man with the sharply defined natural resistance has to have his powers reduced one by one, the man with the

[142] Judg. 6:37-38.

better-poised temperament yields to the same process more simply and comprehensively.

However integrated psychologically, the soul that is to walk in the way of mystical contemplation must be prepared to undergo the trials that were dealt with in the foregoing chapter. In order to say with St. Paul that "if we have known Christ according to the flesh, we now know Him so no longer,"[143] we must have learned our lesson of faith in darkness. It is only in the paradoxical light of darkness that we come to "know God as unknown."[144]

All the soul can do is bring the senses into line. Stilling the overactivity of the faculties, smothering the eccentricities, and directing the desires toward God, the soul must then wait upon the action of grace. "Quietly dwelling in the Word in whom is seen the beginning," is one of St. Augustine's descriptions of contemplative prayer.

Between the soul and its perception of God, there is in this life always a veil of sense. Faith penetrates it, but sight, just because it is itself a sense, does not. "We walk by faith," says St. Paul again, "and not by sight."[145] Confronted with this veil, and filled with the desire to see God, souls can make the darkness deeper for themselves than it is meant to be. They can make it dark to no purpose, unproductive of mystical knowledge and light. Overeagerness — which is only a want of proper balance — can hamper the action of grace and delay the ultimate dawn. So it is while in this state of hunger and

[143] 2 Cor. 5:16.
[144] Cf. Acts 17:23.
[145] 2 Cor. 5:7.

impatience that the soul must know its place, must stay calm on what seems to be the wrong side of the curtain.

The veil must be allowed to hide the face of Christ. Death will take away the curtain — because when this happens, the senses will be taken away with it — but in the meantime there must be faith. The nights of sense and spirit — because they, too, are a form of death — will make the veil of sense increasingly transparent, but even here there is no immediate sight of God. There is knowledge, but not sight.

Only now, when the nights have done their work and drawn the powers of the soul into unity, is there a right understanding of life and love and the service of God generally. "If, then, any be in Christ a new creature, the old things are passed away. Behold all things are made new."[146] Yes indeed, the soul recognizes a new Heaven and a new earth, and the former self is buried with the past.[147]

∽

Likeness to Christ brings your
inner and outer selves into harmony

If it were solely a matter of harmonizing the emotions and quieting their excessive activity in prayer, the matter might be allowed to rest there. But the question is a wider one. The whole man, outward as well as inward in his operation, has to be given to God. Nothing, as the Incarnation itself teaches, may be left out. "Behold the man,"[148] the representative man.

---

[146] Rev. 21:4-5.
[147] Cf. Rev. 21:1.
[148] John 19:5.

Just as those who are afraid of suffering must be shown how to suffer with Christ, so those who are afraid of happiness must be taught how to be happy in Christ. Holiness is not exclusive; it is comprehensive. It is the saint who is the complete man; not the impoverished personality, but the enriched one. The union of divine and human as existing in Christ finds its counterpart in the harmony of natural and supernatural in the life of the saint. In the saint, there are not two lives, one relating to God and one to outward affairs, but a single life — and that in Christ.

With the progressive assimilation of Christ's Spirit, the conflict between the outward and the inward is resolved. The claims of work and prayer are harmonized. The functions of Martha and Mary interact in the single activity of love.[149] It is not that the contemplative does not now much notice or care whether he is employed in active or interior work; it is rather that, having a single principle operating within him, he can confidently take on either without loss to the other. He may vastly prefer one occupation to the other, but his preferences make no difference to his decisions. The qualifying factor is the will of God.

In our problems of reconciling conflicting loyalties, when trying to weld together the duties that seem to us mutually exclusive, we turn for precedent to Christ's life as recounted for us in the Gospels. Here, we realize, the active and the contemplative answer will be blended. There will not be two

---

[149] Martha and Mary, friends of Christ, represent, respectively, the active and contemplative sides of the Christian life; cf. Luke 10:38-42.

pulls, as with us and in opposite directions, but one. From the pages of the Gospel, we get, up to a point, what we are looking for — but perforce only up to a point. Christ's recorded example, confined to occasions that find no more than a rough parallel in our own lives, does not help us as much as we had hoped. This is as it should be. Christ's example was never meant to provide us with a formula; it was meant to provide us with a principle.

If the settings were identical in Christ's life and our own, there would be little merit in our repeating the precedent. If the Mass were *exactly* like the Last Supper and Calvary, the mystery of our Faith would be robbed of half its meaning. It is not the historical performance of Christ's life that has to be acted over again in other ages and other countries; what has to be re-enacted is the exhibition of His love and the significance of His words.

It is in the context of our own circumstances that the Gospel narrative is reproduced. And for this, unavoidably, there has to be a translation. It is precisely in the work of translation that the work of faith comes in. I have to find the application to my particular need. Only so can my reference to the text be of any practical or spiritual use.

It is in the divine-human personality of Christ, then, although perhaps not in any one act or saying of His, that I shall see harmonized the warring elements of my vocation. And this will be not in any abstract Christ, removed from historical actuality and considered only in terms of wisdom and authority, but in the Christ recorded for us by the Evangelists. Adjusted to my mentality and need, all the words Christ has spoken can be brought to my mind. With the Apostles, I must be able to look back and see, in the light of His Spirit, whom the Father has sent in His name, whatsoever He has taught. It is only the scene that has changed; the teaching remains the same.

So here again we find ourselves trying to peer through a curtain that separates us from the clear sight of Him for whom we are looking. We can make out His shadow and hear the echo of His words, but this is as far as we can get. Always in this life we have to rely on forms and symbols. God must still remain a hidden God, or faith and hope would be meaningless and love merely an emotion.

The symbols are true as far as they go, but we are hungering for truth itself. The whole of creation points to truth — "for the invisible things are clearly seen being understood by the things that are made"[150] — but when we are clamoring for the Creator Himself, we are inclined to be foolishly impatient with creation.

We are impatient because we are not properly balanced. If, in the terms of St. Paul's prayer for the Ephesians, Christ dwelt more fully by faith in our hearts,[151] we would be better content with the symbols He chooses for His revelation. Until Christ be more perfectly formed in us — that is, until we have re-flected the harmony that is in Christ — we shall never get the most out of God's external utterance, whether in created form or inspired form, and perhaps we shall even misread it.

It remains for us, then, to continue looking in faith. That is all we can do. But because it is all that God wants, it is enough. "I will wait for the Lord who hath hid His face," says Isaiah,

---

[150] Rom. 1:20.
[151] Eph. 3:17.

"and I will look for Him."[152] And St. Augustine once again, with another description of the contemplative act, speaks of "the soul that learns to direct a straight and serene look toward the object to be gazed at." Straight: no deviations from the immediate range and direction of vision. Serene: unanxious, unquestioning, uncomplicated. This is what is meant by balance.

---

[152] Isa. 8:17.

Chapter Fifteen

Strive for the holiness God desires

Although the desire for God can never be excessive, the desire for the realization of this desire can be excessive. Souls that indulge their hunger for final union with God, or even for immediate satisfaction in God, are like souls that indulge their hunger for anything else. (We are talking of indulgence, that is to say, of feeding an appetite beyond its legitimate demand, and not of taking the means appropriate to the desire.)

Souls misguided by greed for what they conceive to be a spiritual end will either take any means they think will gratify their hunger, or else, deprived of satisfaction, will escape into other satisfactions altogether.

It is only when they have been brought to admit both the necessity of waiting upon God's will until the moment arrives when He is ready to unite Himself with them, and the futility of trying to exploit other appetites in compensation, that such souls can dispose themselves for the union that they so much desire.

In other words, these people have to be detached from overeagerness before they can be rendered smooth enough to receive the imprint of God. Greed implies a lack of unity, and the soul has to be unified before it can be united with the One.

∞

Your spiritual life
must be founded on faith

St. Teresa[153] describes the aberrations of devout souls who imagined that they could not exist for a day without Holy Communion. Here, among St. Teresa's subjects in the convent, were spiritual people hungering for spiritual food — but hungering unduly, and having to be weaned from what was an exaggeration, seeing that they in fact were receiving Holy Communion every day.

What had happened was that these nuns, while genuinely longing for God, had deceived themselves as to the way in which their longing was meant by God to be satisfied. They had the details wrong: the time and the number and the manner had seemed to them all-important. The Holy Eucharist had been understood in terms of its secondary instead of its primary significance. To these nuns, it was not so much the sacrament, but the administration of the sacrament, that mattered; not so much the effect it would have upon the soul, but the effect it would have upon the senses of the soul that made them so eager for its reception.

When we are impatient beyond a certain moment of control, we are more often than not led to take means that are wrong to supply needs that are right. But it works the other way as well: we can be led to take means that are good in order to achieve ends that are bad. All this, in one or the other aspect, has to do with looking for escapes.

---

[153] St. Teresa of Avila (1515-1582), Spanish Carmelite nun and mystic.

So it would appear that, if the work is to be for God, not only must the means be examined in the light of grace, but the need has to be examined, too. For example, there may be a real need, but not a real necessity. Where there is a necessity, there is a corresponding pledge of God's help in meeting it. Where there is a need, there is again the help of God waiting to be asked for; but if the need is of our own making, or if we neglect to ask for God's help in meeting it, there is no guarantee that our effort at solution will receive divine assistance. When we create a need, we have no right to the cooperation of the Creator. When the Creator creates a necessity, we have every right to expect that the Creator will continue His work.

God may be left to see to the supernatural demands that lie in the nature of the human soul. When man begins too actively to take a hand in supplying these demands, he acts according to nature and not according to grace. It does not do to step in front of God.

In the same way, it is a common thing to find spiritual people who try to compensate for their inability to pray as they would like to pray by looking for, and even imagining that they are favored with, extraordinary graces. It is an escape. To expect a vision, let alone to imagine one, is an escape. For the time being, as when the Carmelite nuns wanted to receive our Lord at the earliest possible moment after midnight so as not to miss a minute of His presence during the day, there is something to distract the mind. For such souls, there is something to walk around with instead of faith. The loneliness is lessened — the loneliness of having to go on waiting.

Material men make for themselves material escapes; spiritual men make for themselves spiritual escapes. Just as the worldling must convince himself that alcohol is only a very fleeting solution to his problem, so the interior man must convince himself that the only solution that does not give rise to further problems requiring yet more solutions is that of faith.

The problem, for the spiritual man as for the material man, is ultimately that of loneliness. The worldling feels isolated temperamentally and dares not face himself in solitude; the religious man feels all the same obstacles to communication with his fellow human beings, and experiences in addition an inability to reach an understanding with God. Neither can the religious man face himself until he has learned humility at its source.

Once a man's life is ruled by faith instead of by temporary experiments and expedients, there can be a balance. Faith gives to a man a focal point within himself to which everything about him can be referred. When the worldling has acquired this knowledge in faith, he is a worldling no longer. When the man of faith has lost it, he is a man of faith no longer; he is a worldling. And this is the awful part: we can neglect the graces of God.

∞

You must not run after spiritual heroism

Almost every excess in the spiritual life, then, can be traced to a desire for God that will not wait, to homesickness for a home that we have never been to, but of which we know enough to realize that we shall never be happy anywhere else. God spells for us security, rest, and belonging.

If we thought of God more in the terms of what He has revealed about Himself and less in terms of what we shall feel when we have found Him, we would be less liable to error in our approach. We tend to dwell too long upon the idea of finding rest in Heaven and the sense of permanent belonging; too little upon the idea of Heaven being a Person and our belonging eternally to Him.

It is only the most superficial singularities in a person's service of God that represent the desire to overplay a part. The real singularities that represent a real part are those that spring from an untamed spiritual yearning. These, if not corrected, can lead to false mysticism, heresy, presumption, and despair. It is as serious as that.

The argument, for substantiation of the above, is simply this: nothing so promotes self-deception as undisciplined desire. The appetites can create a sense of urgency and a sense of reality that are quite untrue. Giving himself a liberty to which he has no right, the man who is self-deceived assumes an inside knowledge about all the things that normally call for faith.

It is not that such a man is possessed of insufficient faith. In a sense, he is possessed of too much. He believes where there are no grounds for belief. He has substituted faith in himself for faith in God.

It is not that such a man pays too little attention to the inner voice that tells him what to do. In a sense, he pays too much attention to it — and hears it entirely wrong. He listens only for his own inspiration, not for God's.

Nobody can tell such a man that he is deluded; he knows that the saints have had to endure the same charge. Authority itself may oppose him; but he is ready for that, too. "In the company of the saints and mystics," he says, "I am not subject to ordinary legislation." It is simply, he tells himself sadly, that these material people who criticize him do not understand the ways of the spirit.

There is nobody who is so well-entrenched, or who can take such risks within his entrenchment, as the martyred soul. Where the opinion of others might have inhibited him before, now it seems to uninhibit him. Stimulated by the conception of being one lonely voice raised against the majority opinion, the false apostle of spirituality rises majestically above the clamor.

Such a man canonizes all he does — not only all he stands for (and he may stand for much that is orthodox and right), but also all that he does and plans to do. Congratulating himself upon his idealism, he lets his ardor for God run away with him. He loses his head and has nothing but his heart to put in its place. But by this time, his heart is so unnaturally developed that it can serve no purpose as a guide.

Following the liberty of the other faculties, the imagination runs riot. Mystical favors are claimed. In the confessional and in correspondence of spiritual direction, the gift of discernment of prophecy is confidently assumed. "I live in the supernatural, not in the natural world; the miraculous is in the air I breathe." The life of faith is exchanged for the life of fancy. The normal is despised and the sensational valued.

A soul in this state will look out for the hard thing to do simply because it is hard and not because it is the will of God. A soul in this state is at the mercy of the Devil, who can as easily arrange occasions for the heroic as he can for the diffident. Heroism is a far more dangerous escape than diffidence.

If his bent is toward asceticism, the deviationist saint will be ready to fast until he dies of starvation. Is he not as eager for death as he is for God?

If his bent is prayer, he will escape from people, work, routine, responsibility, and even obedience, in order to generate an atmosphere of recollection. The sad part is that he may get his atmosphere of recollection and this will only confirm him that he was right.

If his bent is hard work, he will sacrifice prayer, charity, prudence, and health in keeping himself busy every moment of the day. Even the worldly man knows the value of work as an escape. If he sees himself as a solitary, he will blast a hole in the wall of his God-given enclosure of existing circumstances, and build for himself a hermitage of his own, where he will sit in bitterness and self-contemplation.

If his hobby is monastic observance, he will scorn the spirit and bow down before the letter. The value of every act will be judged by conformity either to primitive usage or to exact physical performance. Nothing will be taken in relation to God and His love; all will be judged as relating to self and personal predilection.

So hypnotized can a spiritually inclined man become that the impulses that a more worldly-minded person would judge at once to be natural are seen in the false light as movements of grace. Whatever stirs him to fervor is accepted as good, holy, and desirable. The fact that it may stir him also to neglect objective duties is not considered. Where devotion is the sole criterion, a new standard enters in, and values follow quite a different order. Spiritual emotion is a heady wine, and habit-forming. The intoxication that it leads to is all the more destroying because it is not shadowed by the sense of guilt.

Then, by the mercy of God, comes the light of day. With self-discovery comes at last not only a sense of guilt but also, assuming that the light is accepted for what it is, a sense of overwhelming gratitude and love. In the burning glare of grace, which cannot now be mistaken for anything else, the soul sees how the whole of its past has been a mounting delusion. Where other lights shone with a rosy glow, this is the white light of truth. No escape now — or if there is an escape, it is the open-eyed flight directly into the arms of evil. The only alternative to trust in God is annihilation of hope. Either start again, or else finish once and for all.

It must be seldom that a soul is so rooted in obstinacy that the chance of beginning again in the love of God is refused; seldom that the exhaustion and humiliation are so great that cooperation with the new vitality of the Christ-life is denied.

Certainly there can be no question as to the soul's defeat; there is nothing on which self-esteem could fasten itself, nothing that could even help self-esteem to revive. The whole question now is how to make capital out of the defeat, how to make of it a triumph of grace.

Now at last, having been evaded before, the theological virtues are put to the test: faith, hope, and love must pull the soul out of the depths. Humility does not grow naturally out of humiliation, and the one kind of confidence does not switch over immediately to the other. It is a time of suffering because the soul, from sheer habit, looks for escapes and there are none, looks for the sweet waters of refreshment and finds none. The flame passes over the whole of the soul, lighting up the most secret corners and entering into the least movements.

But for once the suffering is not resented; it is seen to be necessary and is gladly endured. "I have deserved this, and I would not be without it," says the soul, "for it is the only way of getting me clean." The attitude is the attitude of the soul in Purgatory — of which it is, happily, a foretaste.

From now on, the soul will know that the service of God is something serious. Its searing experience has shown that spiritual frivolities can never be the objects of a soul's endeavor. When I have the honesty to say, "In my mysticism, I have been a sham; in my direction of others, I have been a common quack; in my asceticism, I have been nothing but a sword-swallower," then there is something on which the new structure of the spiritual life can be built. Sound foundations are now being prepared.

How else, if we are not to be so reduced in our own estimation, can we make room for the All? How else can we be taught the meaning of the love that is stronger than satisfaction and sense? How else can we be stripped of our illusions, save by the process of burning exposure?

Humility, confidence, love, faith: there can be no other preparation for the life of Christ. And when we have said this, we know that these qualities come to us as a gift from Him. "For another foundation no man can lay but that which is laid," says St. Paul to the Corinthians, "which is Christ Jesus."[154]

---

[154] 1 Cor. 3:11.

∝

Chapter Sixteen

Seek to know the Holy Spirit

If God had revealed Himself only as the Father, man would have worshiped in fear and awe, but not so much with love. If He had revealed Himself in the Incarnation only, man would have loved Him in His sacred humanity, but would have found it less easy to worship Him as God. If He had revealed Himself as the Holy Spirit and not as the Father and the Son, man would have made of Him too much an abstraction, and not enough a Person.

In order to counter this misconception of the Third Person of the Blessed Trinity, we do not have to persuade ourselves that He is in fact like the Father and the Son. He is not *like* — He *is*.

To restrict our understanding of the Holy Spirit to a vague concept in which neither the majesty of the Father nor the humanity of the Son finds its place is to know the Holy Spirit incompletely and wrongly. It is to know Him only as a world-wide holy influence, a mysterious power for good.

Now, we must get this right. How must I contemplate the Holy Spirit? What exactly does the Holy Spirit do? Why cannot my salvation depend simply upon the Father's mercy and the Son's atonement? What love can the Holy Spirit give to me, or elicit from me, that cannot equally be mine through the action of the Father and the Son?

Theology teaches us that in the mutual relations of Persons within the Trinity — the generation of the Son by the Father, and the procession of the Holy Spirit from the Father and the Son — the eternal activity of God consists. Theology further teaches that we exist only because God is. With the rest of creation, we owe all that we are to the fact of God's subsistence.

Coming into being through the act of God by which He is of Himself alone, we live and move and are sanctified by that same act. The more we see into the nature of our dependence on the life of the Blessed Trinity, the deeper and truer will our spirituality become. If the whole of human activity, whether of being or becoming, hangs upon its participation in this unceasing generation and procession of Persons, we cannot afford to miss anything that may be taught us about the Spirit who breathes the life of the Trinity into our souls.

Granted that we are what we are because God is who He is, not only will the life of God be communicable to man, but a knowledge of the nature of God will also be communicable to man. Man must be able to know something of the principle of his existence, must be able to know something of God's nature.

In bringing the life of God to us — that is to say, in living His life within us — the Holy Spirit brings us knowledge of Himself. But because our finite minds are incapable of directly assimilating knowledge about the infinite nature of God, we have to learn our knowledge indirectly and by analogy.

The Holy Spirit, then, instructs us by symbols. From what we know of outward things, our minds are directed by the Spirit to the inward. It is in this way that we first come to know, from our experience of relationships within a family, what is meant by God the Father and God the Son. What is meant by God the Holy Spirit, because it is less readily translated into terms of symbol, is less readily perceived.

To come to a knowledge of the part played by the Holy Spirit, either in the external generation and procession of the Blessed Trinity or in the temporal sphere of human existence, we still have to use metaphors and similes, and perhaps less tangible metaphors and symbols than those that served to clarify knowledge of Father and Son, but we have the assurance of the Holy Spirit Himself that our effort at further knowledge will be blessed.

Consubstantial with the Father and the Son, the Holy Spirit is related to us as the Divine Wisdom, who, at once the Father's power and the Son's love, makes us holy. This is not the whole activity of the Spirit, because the Holy Spirit operates in regions beyond that of human personality; nor does it represent the sum of knowable truth about the Holy Spirit, because, as we shall see, there is much more to be learned about Him. It is, however, the aspect of His activity and of His truth that we shall most need to study.

The idea of God the Holy Spirit that has to be conveyed to our minds must be presented so as not only to allow the least margin of error, but, on the positive side, to make for an influence on thought and life. The Holy Spirit does not exist to be a dogma, but to be a Person. The function of Holy Wisdom is to be a live doctrine, an infinitely perfect intelligence speaking to, and in, finite souls.

It is possible for us to restrict the activity of the Holy Spirit within our souls either by turning a deaf ear to the impulses of grace or by assuming that the intelligence of man can know so little of the mysteries of God anyway that it is not worth trying to learn. We do not have to belittle our human intellects; they are small enough already. To stunt their development is to sin against grace. To stunt them on the grounds of humility is laziness and pride.

Souls who neglect to acquire the knowledge to which, in the order of nature as well as in the order of grace, they have a right are not only forfeiting a good, but laying themselves open to an evil.

While we have the light, we must walk.[155] If we fail to make use of the light, or allow it to go out before its time, we walk in darkness. And this will not be the darkness of grace and faith, but the darkness of self and error.

There are truths of faith that, although knowledge of them will forever remain imperfect, can be so inadequately known as to be erroneously known. By taking either too much for granted about the Holy Spirit, or too little, we can be left with a knowledge that does us harm.

We may possess faith and we may possess truth, but we may possess so little of them as not to advance as we should toward the object of faith and the essence of truth. It is the work of the Holy Spirit dwelling within the soul to develop the life of faith and deepen the apprehension of truth. But it is the outward life of faith as well as the inward that has to be brought under the action of the Holy Spirit. It is the apprehension of moral as well as dogmatic truth that has to be learned from the Holy Spirit.

[155] John 12:35.

A one-sided response to the Holy Spirit will simply not do. Where grace is followed in prayer but not in works, there can be no true knowledge of the Holy Spirit. Where the doctrines of Christ are believed but the implications of His doctrine are denied, there can be no true knowledge of the Holy Spirit.

Thus, the more a man comes to know about the person and nature of the Holy Spirit, the more he will come to know about the truths and laws that flow from God.

The faith that is based upon a faulty knowledge of the Holy Spirit will not attain to truth. The conduct that is based on a faulty knowledge of the Holy Spirit will err in morals. The law of God, which both faith and conduct must follow, is the will of God. And the will of God is signified by the Spirit of God — just as the Spirit of God is signified by the will of God — so, for the safety of faith and truth, there must be no lack of knowledge on the part of the soul.

Fortunately, we are supplied by the Fathers, the Doctors, and the theologians of the Church with ample material from which to build up our knowledge of the Holy Spirit. From Holy Scripture and dogmatic theology, we come to know something of His nature; from mystical theology, something of His operation; and from moral theology, something of His demand. These sciences take us a great part of the way, but not all the way.

The last stretch of the way has to be made on the sole reliance, by faith, upon the Holy Spirit Himself. And for this act on our part, the knowledge that is acquired from the various branches of theology will not immediately help us. Indirectly it will help, but not directly.

∞

The Holy Spirit enlightens your soul

The wisdom communicated to man by Wisdom Himself is not a wisdom that can be consciously drawn upon to meet a particular emergency; rather, it is a secret habit of the soul which disposes of the difficulties as they come along, but in such a way that its actual exercise escapes the attention of him through whom the grace of the Holy Spirit is operating.

By the same token, there is an area of spiritual understanding wherein the inconsistences of human life are transcended, and in which the difficulties of faith are met. This area falls within the special province of the Holy Spirit. It might be said that the Holy Spirit is the voice of the Word telling the voices of this world to be quiet so that the truth of the Blessed Trinity, which again is the Spirit and the Word together, may be absorbed.

By surrendering to the way of the Holy Spirit, we open our souls to a new way of apprehending, to a new knowledge. The act that yields becomes one with the act that receives, so that, in the soul that is completely at the disposal of the Holy Spirit, there is an uninterrupted circulation of grace. Where the Holy Spirit has this undisputed direction of a soul, there will gradually emerge a new understanding of the symbols that reveal Him. What were dead words and forms before are now the movements of a living mind. The soul no longer lives in a world of metaphor, but in a world of hidden reality wherein the metaphors are as real as anything else. The analogies do not so much point to reality as express reality.

By the words of a poem, a man is led to see a likeness to things in nature; by poetry he sees into nature. By forms and images, a man comes to see a likeness of God; by the light of the Holy Spirit, he comes to live in the presence of God. Images are not untrue things that resemble truth; they are true things that express truth, but not fully. The symbolic, because it veils the Spirit which gives it meaning, is seen to have an existence and validity that are far from unreal.

Evidence of the Holy Spirit's activity now declares itself a hundred times a day. It is seen in the Mass, in spiritual reading, and in stray conversation. Nor is it only that certain printed sentences or certain spoken words are felt to be directives or eye-openers straight from God Himself — God, as it were, instructing the soul at intervals during the day with precise points of information — but rather, that the work of the Holy Spirit is seen to underlie everything that is, and that all things combine to say the same thing.

The most important part of life, the life of prayer, is still lived in darkness. Here God speaks to us still in riddles — or does not speak to us at all. But for the rest, there is everywhere evidence of His presence; His Spirit is known to be the breath of life. Thus whether the immediate witness comes to us from a phrase in the Liturgy, from an article in St. Thomas, from a flash of light while we are thinking of something else, or from a tree in the garden, all things are found in their origin, which is God.

The lines that seemed so casually introduced into the first act of the play, so unrelated, are remembered when the play has reached its climax. It is while we are watching the third act that their significance is appreciated.

Everywhere one turns, one realizes that the Holy Spirit has been there all along. In each emergency as it arises, one knows that the Holy Spirit has the solution — and He alone has the solution. In every decision that one has to make, one trusts more and more that the Holy Spirit is making it for him.

One is now not so much confronted with instances that prove the existence of God's presence either in one's own affairs or in the universe at large, but rather, one is confronted with God who proves that He is present in the instances. Under the progressive activity of grace, one comes to find a certain familiarity about the world in which one's outward and inward life is now lived — as if one had been here before, in some previous existence. It is as though life in this rediscovered world had at some time been divided into two and was now being made one again. The unfamiliar is felt to be familiar after all. The old things are made new, and the new things, because they are seen in terms of the old, are even made true and real and right. They are seen as the things of God.

A one-time inhabitant of a submerged city, coming back in an afterlife and looking down through the clear water from the side of a boat, would not have to be reminded that such-and-such a person had lived there years ago, that these and those goods had been sold in the shops, that the rulers of the city had pursued a certain policy, and that the university had specialized in the study of a certain subject. The dead city, to that revenant, would live.

In the same way, the man who has come to life again in the Holy Spirit does not have to make an effort of the imagination — any more than the other has to make an effort of the memory — to see that dwelling here in this submerged city of everyday life are the infallible truths of the Church, the doctrines of theology, the individual members of the Mystical

Body of Christ and the whole body itself, our Lady and all the saints.

Such a soul sees all this by the mere act of keeping his eyes open. If he responds to the grace of the Holy Spirit, he cannot miss these things. Indications of the Spirit are normal to him because the norm of his life has been transferred from the material to the spiritual. The Holy Spirit is in the city that he is looking at and in him whose eyes are turned toward it, and there is now an affinity that was not appreciated before.

Never suggesting that God and His creation are one, which would be heresy, nor that God is perceived without the effort to make the act of faith, we can see how a soul may come eventually to have a very clear perception of God in the created order — although refracted in the element of perception.

While we are alive on earth, we can have no other vision of God than that which is according to our disposition in receiving it. Since our disposition is limited by our mortal nature, we are bound to be separated from Him and from the city of our desire by an element to which we are naturally akin. But as the Holy Spirit reveals Himself to us, we come to see through this element. Or, if you like, we come to see in it everywhere His reflection.

Just as He has shown Himself to us as Man — yet obscurely, because we must see in Him more than Man — so He shows Himself to us as Spirit — again obscurely. In the Holy Spirit, we worship Him in whom dwells the fullness of the Godhead.[156]

Just as Christ teaches us with the words that He preached while on earth and with the infallible voice that speaks to us

---

[156] Col. 2:9.

through the Church, so the Holy Spirit teaches us with the graces that make us understand those words and obey that voice.

He is the Spirit of wisdom, truth, revelation, and knowledge, revealing to us the mysteries of faith and the attributes of God. It is He who directs us in the way of life and preserves us from illusion, error, apathy, and deception. "Thou art the true light and divine fire, O master of souls," sings St. Augustine in the *Soliloquies*, "and as the Spirit of truth, Thou teachest us all truth through Thy communication."

Chapter Seventeen

Allow the Holy Spirit
to sanctify you

The extent to which the souls of the blessed in Heaven rejoice
in the Holy Spirit we can only guess. All we know is that
their happiness in the Blessed Trinity is measured by the extent to which they have believed, hoped, and loved on earth.
And since, for the exercise of the theological virtues, souls on
earth require the grace of the Holy Spirit, we may guess that
gratitude to the Holy Spirit is not the least of the joys of
Heaven.

Although the factor that distinguishes the Church Triumphant from the Church Militant[157] is the absence of faith and
hope in the Church Triumphant, it is in the activity of love
that the Holy Spirit is just as much occupied. If Heaven is
love, life on earth should be a preparation in love. Even if it
were not His work to develop faith and hope among the faithful, the Holy Spirit would be as closely related to us as the Father and the Son in the development of our love.

---

[157] The Church Triumphant comprises all the members of the
Church in Heaven, and the Church Militant, the members
on earth.

The possession of God, in which the joy of the blessed essentially consists and which is nothing other than love made absolute, can in its degree be experienced even on earth. The substantial good of Heaven can be anticipated in this life according to the measure of growth in the grace of the Holy Spirit.

The soul's growth in the Holy Spirit is therefore the whole secret of life: the life of Christ in the soul, the virtues, the gifts — all is assumed in the possession of, and response to, the action of the Holy Spirit. Without the continuous action of the Holy Spirit, we cannot "grow in grace and knowledge of our Lord and Savior Jesus Christ."[158] Without His inspiration, we cannot call upon the name of Jesus, let alone follow His teaching. Without His crowning grace of sanctification, we cannot enter Heaven.

If, in order to reach maturity in Christ, we need His Spirit at every step of the way, the process by which we learn the life of Christ will not be one primarily of intellectual endeavor; primarily it will be one of response to grace. Intellect and imagination can only reconstruct the life of Christ; it requires the Holy Spirit to reproduce it in us.

The "attainment of perfect manhood in Christ"[159] will never be fully realized until we get to Heaven, but there is a reaching out toward the "plenitude of God"[160] that not only *may* be begun on earth, but *must* be begun and developed if we are to enjoy eternal life. If we do not grow, we become feeble

[158] 2 Pet. 3:18.
[159] Cf. Eph. 4:13.
[160] Cf. Eph. 3:19.

and die. Our life, seen as the life of grace on earth and eternal life in Heaven, depends on the Holy Spirit.

This is why the Holy Spirit is called the Sanctifier. By His action in us, we lay hold on eternal life. "This is eternal life, that they may know Thee and Jesus Christ whom Thou hast sent."[161] We learn about the Father and the Son by the light of the Spirit, and so already here on earth we possess the beginnings of eternal life.

The sanctification that we receive from the Holy Spirit is not like a token offering, a goodwill gift bestowed from above in virtue of the infinite perfection of God, but rather is like the penetration of one nature by another. "Just as iron thrown into the midst of a fire receives the nature of fire," says St. Basil,[162] "and in its color, heat, and activity is changed into fire; so by reason of the communion which they have with Him who is holy by His very nature, the powers of the soul receive His entire substance and possess, as it were, an innate sanctification."

Our sanctification is not our own; it is borrowed. Rather, it is assimilated, absorbed. It becomes not so much an offshoot of divine perfection (which again would imply pantheism) as an inclusion in it.

We are not so much like beggars holding out an empty tin for a rich man to drop a coin into it, as like those whose poverty is assumed into, and swallowed up by, infinite wealth.

We are not so much like lepers waiting for the doctor to come with his ointment to dress the sores; we are more like the

[161] John 17:3.
[162] St. Basil (c. 330-379), Bishop and Doctor.

sores themselves, taken upon Him who bore our infirmities, and so finding health.

We are not like the hungry looking for a meal that will keep them from starvation; rather, we are consumed by Him who Himself is prepared to be our food.

"The difference between them and the Holy Spirit is this," concludes St. Basil, still speaking of the human powers that receive sanctification in the fact of communication with the divine nature, "that in the Spirit is holiness by nature, whereas sanctification is in them by participation."

In the letter to the Ephesians, the Christian soul is referred to as "a habitation of God in the Spirit";[163] in the first letter to the Corinthians, as "the temple of God in whom the Spirit of God dwells." "For the temple of God is holy, which you are,"[164] St. Paul goes on. "Know you not," he asks, "that your members are the temple of the Holy Spirit who is in you, whom you have from God, and that you are not your own?"[165]

In these texts, we have the pledge of divine life and divine direction. While remaining ourselves, we do not belong to ourselves. We are not our own but His who remains within us. St. Paul's words point to the fulfillment of our Lord's promise to His disciples immediately before His arrest in the garden: "I will ask the Father, and He will give you another Paraclete, that He may abide with you forever. The Spirit of truth . . . shall be in you."[166]

[163] Eph. 2:22.
[164] Cf. 1 Cor. 3:16, 17.
[165] 1 Cor. 6:19.
[166] John 14:16-17.

But we see from the same chapter of St. John that there is a condition attached to this promise: "He that hath my commandments and keepeth them. . . . If anyone love me, he will keep my word."[167] Obedience and charity, then, make possible the indwelling of the Spirit: a rejection of the commandments — any of them and not only the first and greatest of the commandments, which is to love — forbids it. Charity and obedience, themselves gifts of God, make holy the temple of God. Charity could not exist *without* obedience. If our love for God is true, we must mean to do what He wants.

It amounts to this: endowed with the actual love with which the Father loves the Son and the Son loves the Church ("I am in the Father and you in me and I in you. . . . He who loveth me shall be loved of my Father, and I will love him"[168]), we find within ourselves the strength to keep the commandments, to live the life of faith, and — most blessed of all — to love back. This power that we possess, "the power to be made the sons of God," is held out to "those who believe in His name" — that is, to those who receive Him on His terms. Receiving Him thus, "as many as receive Him" are made sharers of His "grace and truth"[169] of which He Himself is the plenitude.

∞

The Holy Spirit increases grace in your soul
Coming somewhat down to earth, we can see now that it is no credit to us when we make decisions according to the

[167] John 14:21, 23.
[168] John 14:20-21.
[169] John 1:12, 14.

Spirit, give advice according to the Spirit, or preach and teach and write according to the Spirit. We are mere witnesses to the truth, mere pipelines of grace. Woe to us if, privileged as we are, we do not perform these services to the Spirit.

By the sheer grace of God, we are what we are.[170] Let us not talk about merit. What do we have that we have not received? The thoughts that we scatter so lavishly abroad — dare we claim that they are our own?

If we do so dare, we make ourselves the source of our own inspiration. However spontaneous our invention, it is only a discovering of what is already there by the creative wisdom of God. The Spirit has been brooding over the waters,[171] stirring the winds of Heaven, supporting the sky, holding the universe in an eternal thought, and here I am talking about "my ideas."

Theology teaches that the sanctifying grace of the Holy Spirit, given the goodwill of the subject and unless interrupted in its action by sin, continues all the time to increase in the soul. Even when a man is asleep, his soul, which is always awake if it is not dead in sin, advances according to the degree of his charity toward further union with God. Such is the effect of his kinship with God in the Spirit that the more purely a man works for God — that is, the more immediately he responds to the impulse of the Holy Spirit — the more closely he forms himself in the likeness of Christ. And the more he develops in the likeness of Christ, the more purely his works are performed. And so it goes on.

[170] Cf. 1 Cor. 15:10.
[171] Cf. Gen. 1:2.

Each act that proceeds from the will of the Christian soul, whether the act relates to the exterior or interior life and whether it is willed explicitly or implicitly, develops the life of grace. And grace enriches the act. Again, so it goes on.

In the element of love, unchallenged in the sanctified soul, the gifts of the Holy Spirit find their fullest expression. In such an environment, all things now work together for good. There is no limit to the expansion of charity, and everywhere there is acknowledgment of the Spirit as the source of all. The gifts do not have to be summoned one by one; the fruits do not have to be examined and worked through in the order of their excellence; the needs to which the light of the Holy Spirit must be sought in remedy do not have to be cataloged. All is seen to be attending upon the Word; the Spirit is felt to be breathing through everything that is.

It is true, of course, that a man will often find himself in an emergency that calls for specific direction from the Holy Spirit. On such an occasion, he should pray to the Holy Spirit, and he can count upon divine help being brought to bear. Choices will have to be made, illusions will have to be exploded, temptations will have to be met, and fears and doubts will have to be dispelled. The gifts will come into play; the fruits will bring confirmation.

But in all this, the influence of the Holy Spirit will be seen rather as a directing and protecting Providence than as an authority to be relied upon to issue *ad hoc* directives. We must avoid superstition in our devotion to the Holy Spirit.

If we approach the Holy Spirit as we would approach an inquiry office, we shall prove not only that our relationship has more in it of self than of love, but also that we have missed His essential function in regard to man — let alone in regard to the Father and the Son within the Blessed Trinity.

The Holy Spirit does not exist solely to provide us with solutions to our problems and doubts. His answer to our necessity is not couched in a formula. The Holy Spirit does not exist solely to conduct us from the lower degrees of prayer to the higher. The Holy Spirit is Love, and whatever we learn of prayer, we learn not so much at His dictation as *in Him*. Love is at once our teacher, our medium, and our life. This is the work of the Holy Spirit.

The Holy Spirit does not exist solely even to "bring all things to our minds whatsoever Christ has said to us."[172] This is only one of His functions. When He receives cooperation and hospitality, it is natural that He should remind the soul of the things that He has said in the Person of Christ. The Paraclete is the Comforter and Teacher and Healer, but so far as we are concerned, He is still more significantly the Sanctifier: He is Holiness Himself and the Third Person of the Blessed Trinity.

"There are diversities of operations," says St. Paul to the Corinthians, "but the same God who worketh all in all. . . . All these things the same Spirit worketh."[173] Beyond all our inquiries, in all our activities, lies the Spirit of Wisdom and Love. Running through every created diversity is the single unifying principle of love. And here, essentially, is the Holy Spirit.

According to Pope Leo XIII,[174] the Third Person in the Blessed Trinity is called the *Holy* Spirit not only because He is

---

[172] Cf. John 14:26.

[173] 1 Cor. 12:6, 11.

[174] Leo XIII (1810-1903), Pope from 1878.

holy by essence, but because He is sanctifying holiness. He is hypostatic charity made actual in the souls of men. "Being supreme love, He directs souls to true sanctity, which consists precisely in the love of God."

Apart from God Himself, all are *made* holy: He alone has the source of sanctity within Himself. The Holy Spirit has no need of grace. He possesses sanctity by nature.

In the process of acquiring our reflected perfection, we come increasingly to focus our attention upon divine truth and beauty. Nothing else is felt to matter, and all that happens takes its value from that. The transformation that is taking place in our lives is a strictly interior one. If the shape of the exterior world is felt to change, it is only because, under the influence of the Spirit, we are changing within. We are being refashioned so that our perceptions focus differently.

Growth in the Spirit means a significant change in perspective: measurements are transferred from the natural to the supernatural. And at first nothing seems to fit. But when, as in the process of printing with more than one block, the technique is grasped and the operation is working smoothly, the outlines are seen to coincide. There is no overlapping. The physical and the spiritual, the temporal and the eternal, the outward and the inward: all come together within the one frame, which is God. Love is the explanation of everything.

"Behold all is made new."[175] The old conflicts have passed away, the inconsistencies are reconciled, and the divided allegiances come together. The Spirit is the bond of peace.[176] It is

---

[175] Cf. 2 Cor. 5:17.
[176] Cf. Eph. 4:3.

only in the knowledge imparted by the Spirit that man may find a synthesis for which no human formula exists.

From what has been said, it will be seen that the Holy Spirit inhabits the soul in much the same way as the Son inhabits the soul. Theology is only echoing Scripture when it describes the manner of divine indwelling. But it is worth observing here that St. Thomas sees a distinction between the presence of one who is given and the presence of one who is sent. "The Holy Spirit is possessed by man and dwells within him," he says, "the very gift itself of sanctifying grace. Hence the Holy Spirit is given and sent." The mission of the Holy Spirit, then, adds something even to the gift.

∞

The Holy Spirit makes you a child of God

"You shall receive the gift of the Holy Spirit,"[177] St. Peter is recorded as saying in the Acts. "And because you are sons," says St. Paul, evidently bringing the relationship into even closer intimacy, "God has sent the Spirit of His Son into your hearts, crying, 'Abba, Father.' "[178]

Certainly the above idea is borne out when we turn to what our Lord Himself said of the Paraclete's mission: "The Holy Spirit, whom the Father will send in my name, will teach you all things. . . . When the Paraclete comes whom I will send you from the Father, the Spirit of truth who proceedeth from the Father, He shall give testimony of me. . . . If I go not, the Paraclete will not come to you, but if I go, I will send Him

[177] Acts 2:38.
[178] Gal. 4:6.

to you."[179] Surely there is a special significance attached to the word *send*: even within the closeness of the indwelling, there is a mission that belongs specifically to the Holy Spirit.

Without putting the faithful under obligations of faith, the Fathers and Doctors of the Church like to ascribe activities proper to each of the Divine Persons. The technical term for this is *appropriation*: attributes common to the three Persons are applied to one by appropriation. Assigned particularly to the Holy Spirit are charity, goodness, peace, and joy.

In the divine indwelling, therefore, each Person of the Blessed Trinity exercises His own proper action upon the soul and promotes sanctification according to His specific and personal communication. The basis for the soul's relationship to any one of the three Persons, and for its claim upon the operation of their attributes, is the initial grace of adoptive sonship.

Furthermore, it is the teaching of theologians that this filiation is not just a matter of initiation — an instantaneous act that produces a certain effect and stops short at that — but is continuous and increasing in activity. Like the subsequent work of sanctification, the adoption that places the soul among the members of the divine household is a grace that accumulates grace.

It is as though a child could become *more* of a son, *more* of a daughter. In the measure that we respond to the grace of filiation, we renew — or rather, we have renewed for us — the grace that started the whole thing off. The mystics speak of regeneration, rebirth, reconception, and reanimation. Words can take us no nearer than this. All we know is that, in the

---

[179] John 14:26, 15:26, 16:7.

sense of St. John's first chapter, God engenders us to His own life through Jesus Christ our Lord.

In a decree at its sixth session, the Council of Trent stated that baptized souls, "having been thus justified and made friends and domestics of God, advancing from virtue to virtue, are *renewed day by day* by the observance of the command-ments of God and the Church. They grow in the justice they have received, and they are further justified. For it is written, 'He who is justified, let him be justified still,' and in another place, 'Do not fear to progress in justice even until death.' "

The parallel between the above quotation and the passages already cited from St. John's Gospel is striking. It is not merely a matter of being born; it is a matter of being faithful. "Of His own will He has begotten us by the word of truth," says St. James in his first chapter, "that we might be some beginning of His creature."[180] That is the beginning; now there must be cooperation.

∞

The Holy Spirit
enkindles love in your soul

When we pray that the Holy Spirit should "fill the hearts of the faithful and kindle in them the fire of His love," we are using the symbol that, among all the symbols of communica-tion, is the most exact. All the rest imply either changing something into something else or the action of one thing upon another from without. Fire is the only element that consumes and transforms into itself.

[180] James 1:18.

The Holy Spirit is the fire of charity which burned up the Apostles from the moment of Pentecost, when it kindled in them the flames of divine love until there was no longer any love of self left in their souls. "Our God is a consuming fire."[181]

The crowning of this act, and the realization of the first part of the prayer to the Holy Spirit, "Fill the hearts of the faithful," will be dealt with in the next chapter.

[181] Heb. 12:29.

Chapter Eighteen

Deepen your knowledge of God

So as not to leave it in the realms of theory and speculation, we can consider this subject from two angles. First, what do the scholastics mean by the *lumen gloriae* ("light of glory"), which is the consummation of the Holy Spirit's work in the soul? Second, how does the soul, under the action of the Holy Spirit, anticipate in this life what in its fullness is reserved for the next?

To arrive at an idea of what the blessed see in Heaven, it is best to dwell for a moment on what the blessed do not see. The Beatific Vision does not mean that God is seen exhaustively. No finite mind, even glorified in Heaven, can comprehend completely an object that is infinite. Nor do the blessed contemplate God by means of images, as we do on earth. St. Thomas says that if the saints saw God through representations only, they could not be said to see Him at all. There can be nothing figurative in the ultimate vision of God. Where there is imagery or created likeness, there cannot be absolute reality. And whatever it is that the blessed in Heaven see of God must be absolutely real.

Now, on the positive side: it is defined that the just shall see God, and see Him face to face. What exactly does this mean? It seems to contradict what has just been said above, but since it cannot do this, we must give the theologians a hearing.

Against the Beghards[182] it has been declared at the Council of Vienna that the souls of the blessed will contemplate the divine essence clearly and intuitively and without any obstacle or intermediary. This is about as much as we can claim. Theologians are still bothered about the nature of the light by which we see all this, and about the process by which the vision is achieved.

Obviously it is neither by reason nor by faith that God is known in Heaven. The knowledge must be immediate or not at all. Processes of abstraction and deduction have no place in Heaven.

What does this leave us?

It leaves us with having to postulate a new power that sees God in a way in which God was not at all seen while the soul was struggling along by the way of faith and hope and argument during the time of its exile on earth. The power or faculty now predicated is immeasurably more perceptive than the corresponding potentiality that has been operating until now. Although the intellect is the same, it is now enlightened so as to apprehend in a different manner and in a different dimension.

Compare the difference in sight between the man before and after being taught how to look at beauty. Compare the

---

[182] The Beghards were members of religious communities founded in the Netherlands in the twelfth century whose social doctrines and mysticism led them to be suspected of heresy by the Church.

difference in hearing between the man before and after being taught the principles of music. Compare the difference of appreciation, joy, and understanding between the man who has learned what literature is about and the man who reads for information.

Now, in order that the finite mind may be receptive to the concept of divinity, a substantial change must take place. The capacity of the soul must be enlarged. This is where the activity of the Holy Spirit comes in. This is where we can turn back to the soul's experience on earth. As a practical problem, then, it comes to this: how much of the *lumen gloriae* can the human soul take in? How far can the response to the Holy Spirit in this life be any sort of rehearsal of the reality that will be experienced in the next?

It should be assumed as axiomatic that unless divinity be dragged down to human knowability, our combined earthly faculties must be made capable, here and now, of true supernatural knowledge. Since we cannot raise them ourselves to the required plane of perception, we rely on the power of the Holy Spirit.

If this were not the case, there would be little enough for the Holy Spirit to do. Were man able, of his own strength, to mount to the vision of the promised land, the Holy Spirit would not have to be responsible for the enlightenment of mankind.

If man could put himself in the way of seeing God face-to-face in Heaven without the aid of the Holy Spirit, there would be no relation between God and man on earth. The whole system of grace and faith and love depends upon the complete and utter insufficiency of man.

Allowing the principle of "whatsoever is received is received according to the dispositions of the recipient"[183] we must allow that in the case of the vision of God, it will be the recipient, not the object received, that will have to change from one plane of being to another. It is the work of the Holy Spirit to bring this change about.

Now then: "None can receive the inheritance of that land of the blessed unless he be moved and led thereto by the Holy Spirit. Therefore, in order to accomplish this end, it is necessary to have the gift of the Holy Spirit." This comes from St. Thomas, and if it tells us anything, it tells us that we can start inheriting now. The land of inheritance is there; the gift of inheritance is here. It is not a matter of geography, but of grace.

If Heaven is nothing more or less than God so presenting Himself to the affective powers of the soul as to be intuitively (which can be taken to mean immediately) known and loved, and if this loving knowledge is guaranteed eternally, what is to prevent such a presentation — all allowances and distinctions appropriate to our human order being taken for granted — from partial realization even in this life?

Once we admit that the human soul is capable of inclusion within the act of the Blessed Trinity, neither the time factor nor the manner of conception need stand in the way. "This is eternal life, that they should know Thee" and if we truly know Thee, Lord, we are in Heaven now.

---

[183] "The fruits of the sacraments . . . depend on the disposition of the one who receives them," *Catechism of the Catholic Church*, no. 1128.

In this life, we shall never possess God in a comprehensive and absolutely intelligible form. But neither shall we in the next. It is the Thomist opinion that in Heaven the divine essence itself takes the place of the absolutely comprehensible. Cannot the process of substitution be begun while the soul is still living on earth?

It is true enough that "eye hath not seen nor ear heard, nor hath it entered into the heart of man to conceive what is in store"[184] for those who love God here below, but the fact that we love Him here below, and know Him even so remotely, is a pledge — and a pledge in kind — of our fuller love and knowledge later on.

It is true that the human intellect relies upon ideas in the building of its knowledge — it cannot know God apart from ideas — but our ideas do nevertheless reveal Him. They are what He uses in us. "I do not wish my *thoughts* of Thee instead of Thee," but if my thoughts of Thee are true and as full as my capacity allows, I am far from bad off: I possess already the elements of eternal life.

For the divine essence to become an intelligible species to a human intellect, the disposition of the understanding mind has to be supernaturally raised. But in the mystical life, this is precisely what happens. It happens only in part, but at least it happens. In part only is the divine substance seen, but at least it is seen. Our knowledge is not illimitable, but at least it is real. "The Spirit searcheth all things, yea the deep things of God. . . . The things that are of God no man knoweth but the Spirit of God. Now, we have received the Spirit that is of

---

[184] 1 Cor. 2:9.

God. . . . For who hath known the mind of the Lord? . . . But we have the mind of Christ."[185]

It may be asked what good the promise of this knowledge does to the man who is floundering about among created representations of God. If he cannot think of God without the medium of sensible association, why hold out any other sort of knowledge at all? Would it not be better, instead of confusing his mind with the theology of being able to see God face-to-face in Heaven and yet not to know Him comprehensively, to let him think of Heaven not as a vision and knowledge, but simply as happiness and rest?

The answer to this is twofold. First, where truth is proposed to the mind of man, the mind of man must grasp as much of it as can be grasped. The more we know of God, although we can never know *all*, the more are we inclined to pray, love, and serve.

To give glory to God, we must have knowledge of God. When our minds are entirely filled with the knowledge of God — that is, when the Holy Spirit has brought His work in us to consummation — the praise we give to God is perfect. Since full praise cannot come out of an empty mind, the more our human reason is trained and stocked with knowledge in this life, the more material we possess with which to worship.

Indeed, this is the purpose of finite knowledge, speculative theology, created wisdom — simply that God be served by the progressively enlightened soul. Knowledge for the sake of knowledge has no supernatural value; the whole value of knowledge lies in the direction of its act.

[185] 1 Cor. 2:10-12, 16.

A man who knows and does not love is like a man who studies a map, reads the literature of the travel agents, obtains a passport, takes his ticket, and then stays at home.

If the little that I know about God at this moment is all that my brain can assimilate, I am in the right way. If I use that little, the grace of the Holy Spirit will lead me on to know more. "Open Thou my eyes," begs the psalmist, "and I will consider the wondrous things of Thy law. . . . Make me to understand the way of Thy justifications. . . . I have chosen the way of truth."[186] When my soul has attained to the light of glory, I shall know the truth of the verses: "Thy justifications were the subject of my song in the land of my pilgrimage. In the night, I have remembered Thy name, O Lord, and have kept Thy law. Thy testimonies are justice forever; give me understanding, and I shall live."[187]

I must not, then, in the sense of the obligation suggested above, limit the extent of my understanding by proposing to myself alternative incentives to the gaining of Heaven. Everyone, the layman and the child no less than the priest and the religious, must respond to the Holy Spirit's work of education.

A novice may not choose to remain in the novitiate when, in the terms of his vocation, a fuller spiritual life awaits him under vows. An acorn may not decide that the wider experience of the oak is to be rejected in favor of the more limited, yet true, existence of the acorn. A stream may not flow on always as a stream if the course open to it is the course of a river.

[186] Ps. 118:18, 27, 30 (RSV = Ps. 119:18, 27, 30).
[187] Ps. 118:54-55, 144 (RSV = Ps. 119:54-55, 144).

∞

Every heart yearns for God

The second answer to the question as to why so much stress is laid upon the knowledge of God in Heaven, when other considerations admit of easier explanation and might make for greater appeal, is that this particular kind of knowledge assumes every other desire.

Although man may not here and now realize that he is looking for the knowledge and vision of God, he is in fact looking for exactly this. A man may tell you that he asks nothing more of Heaven than that he should be eternally among those whom he has loved on earth. Another may want of Heaven the realization of noble ambitions or enlightened ideals. Another may see it as the limitless enjoyment of beauty, repose, and achievement.

But if you take a hundred men, each with his own idea of Heaven, you will find agreement on one thing: eternal bliss must involve the exclusion of every possible dissatisfaction. And, indeed, on any showing, Heaven in other terms would be unthinkable.

What does this amount to? It means that what every human mind is yearning for is the Absolute. In whatever obscure way we grope toward it, whatever devious paths we follow, we all crave the whole good that shall not be taken away from us. It has to be whole, and it has to be everlasting. And, of course, it has to be good.

The created intellect cannot not desire this. When, in his human affairs, a man chooses away from the good, the true, the beautiful, and the lasting, he is not strictly escaping from this law of his nature, but mistaking it. He has made for himself a bad thing into a good. He has forced himself into a self-deception, and then he has let his free will choose wrong.

Allowing for every difference of natural taste and supernatural bent, the principle is universal that every man desires the same good. This good is ultimately nothing else but happiness in God. In the measure that the light of the Holy Spirit is admitted to the soul, the mind is disabused of its false notions of the good, of happiness. Those differentiating wants — although, for most, they were hardly more than wishes — that were seen to give some sort of substance to the idea of Heaven are now unified into a single desire. It is as if the Holy Spirit, acting like the flame of a blowtorch, were to burn away the superficial and disclose at last the real. As the mural decorations peel off, the beauty of the structure appears.

The process may involve pain (either here or, more obviously, in Purgatory), but the process of acquiring knowledge is always painful. There may be a sense of loss, of frustration, or of bewilderment; but when the light has done its work, the reason for the awkwardness of the operation will appear. Then, when the new wisdom has been learned, the original conceptions of Heaven will be seen as childish fancies.

The whole thing now is God — nothing else. He is the whole good and the only good. Nothing matters now but the deeper knowledge and clearer vision of Him. To know Him alone is to know all and to see all. In this is found the triumph of the Holy Spirit in the soul.

An attempt has been made in these three chapters on the Holy Spirit to trace the soul's progress in grace. Whatever advance is made by the soul is made in charity through the Holy Spirit. That this treatment of the subject is no novelty, we

How to Find God

have as witness a number of Fathers whose method provides us with precedent as well as material. "The Father is the fount, the Son is the river, and the Holy Spirit is that from which we drink," says St. Athanasius, "and drinking the Holy Spirit, we drink also Christ." By means of the Word, says St. Irenaeus,[188] we are carried by the Holy Spirit to the Father, for whom our souls thirst.

And that this life in the Trinity is nothing else but the life of charity, we have the familiar passage from St. Augustine: "The beginning of charity is the beginning of justification; progress in charity is progress in justification; and perfect charity is perfect justification."

So it is that when charity is perfected in us — that is to say, when the Holy Spirit has taught us all that our capacity can contain — we shall come to see God revealed as He really is, Infinite Goodness, and we shall know then that the sum of all our desires has found its object in Him and could never have found its objective anywhere else.

[188] St. Irenaeus (c. 130-c. 200), Bishop of Lyons.

Chapter Nineteen

Learn to judge
by the light of God

If God alone can answer the exigency of the human soul, and
if man can confuse his own need so far as to imagine that it can
be satisfied by one or another of a whole catalog of joys, the
immediate demand will be for the gift of discernment. A man
must be able to distinguish between the absolutely and the relatively important.

The power to discern between means and end, between
real and superficial, between holy and very nearly holy, springs
from a number of gifts: it is a combination of knowledge, wisdom, and understanding.

Although predominantly a supernatural quality — in this
context, at any event, for if it is to be of any use in the spiritual
life, it must find its origins in the Holy Spirit — it is nevertheless partly the fruit of natural experience. It is not one of the
specific gifts of the Holy Spirit.

Or put it this way: the ability to discern — allowing that it
is not immediately infused, as in some cases it manifestly is —
grows out of natural happenings planned to a supernatural
end. It is acquired in the dark night of the soul, which brings
spiritual maturity. It is the result of grace working on nature.

That outward circumstances play a part in the formation of a spiritual judgment may be seen by merely looking at the kind of circumstances that interior souls at one time or another have to face. It is easy enough to estimate the effect of these things upon their characters. Loss of material goods conduces to a man's discernment. With detachment from outward standards comes a greater reliance upon the significance of the inward.

Sickness conduces to discernment. There is nothing like a long illness to teach a man the difference between true and false compassion. If only from the sight of his own self-pity, he learns the value of entering into the pains of others.

Suffering of every kind — and especially the suffering of temptation — fosters the potentiality of discernment. Not only is the genuine need distinguished from the sham, but even in the need that is unjustified, that is brought upon itself, an element of sincerity can be discovered that demands an act of understanding.

Solitude ministers to discernment. Sometimes it is born in it. In fact, one wonders how a soul can come to possess the discerning spirit without the help of solitude and silence.

And, above all, prayer: in the practice of unrelenting prayer, hours of it and carried on over the years, a soul chiefly learns to judge according to the spirit. Discernment is nothing other than this: the power to interpret God. How, short of the directly miraculous, can God's will be interpreted as it is capable of being interpreted apart from the light of prayer?

We do not pray in order to discern between the *this* and *that* of every day; we pray in order to please God. But unless we pray, it is unlikely that we shall be able to discern anything according to God. It is in the climate of prayer and against the background of prayer that the outlines appear. Out of the mists, the claims declare themselves. And it is in virtue of prayer that we have the grace to see, the wisdom to decide, and the strength to meet.

Although it is true to say that prayer, and particularly the prayer of darkness as experienced in the nights of sense and spirit, makes for the quality of discernment, it has nevertheless to be admitted that souls of prayer may be found who are wanting in this particular kind of spiritual perception. Where this is the case, it is not that the power has been denied to the soul, but that the soul has been so preoccupied with other things as not to notice and accept it. For example, if the focus of the prayer has been upon self and not upon God, the secondary benefits of prayer will not be valued. And among them is the grace of being able to focus the light of true judgment upon the affairs either of self or of God — let alone upon the affairs of other people.

It would be just the same if the soul misappropriated any of the other contributing causes: to reject the grace of suffering, solitude, sickness, or poverty is to close the soul to a particular area of possible activity. The light of the Spirit must penetrate to every part if the powers of the soul are to reflect that light.

When the powers of the soul have been trained in their supernatural activity, and the training takes place in the nights of sense and spirit, the grace of discerning the things of God must follow. The things of self, the things of the world, the things of the Devil — these things stand out a mile. But it does presuppose, all this, that the work of the nights has really been successful.

Whether finding its object outside the soul, as in counsel and compassion, or in the purely interior field, as when facing personal self-deception or sifting true and false motives, this expression of the gift of understanding is seen to depend upon two factors: detachment and truth. These are — again under cultivation of the Holy Spirit — the conditions of direct perception.

∞

Giving and receiving spiritual
direction requires discernment

Assuming that it is only the detached mind that can be relied upon for a completely objective judgment, the detachment must be spiritual as well as physical. The only sure disposition for the weighing of spiritual balances is a foundation that is itself spiritually even. A weighing machine that tilts to one side or cannot be kept still must inevitably register according to its particular fault. Allowance has to be made for this in the final calculation. A soul swayed by a spiritual fad, and, still more, a soul that moves restlessly from fad to fad, will never be sure of reading the needle correctly.

The work of giving spiritual direction, which should be nothing else but that of drawing upon the gifts of counsel and understanding, will not be fruitful if conducted on a system of slogans. To apply a fixed and favorite principle indiscriminately is not to allow room for the significant action of direction that comes from the Holy Spirit. If one man is to help another in the spiritual life, there has to be a certain flexibility on both sides; each must be prepared to recognize the mediated will of God. The bond between such souls is a spiritual one, and to communicate at the level of the doctrinaire is to turn it into an intellectual one.

To approach any spiritual problem in a particular frame of mind is to rule out the necessity of discernment. Such an approach would be profitable only where either the mind or the frame had been made up by grace — in which case there would be no great problem to approach. Since what we are considering here is not the obedience to a law — for where advice about this has to be given, there should certainly be a frame of mind in the approach — but the resolving of a spiritual difficulty, we can ask ourselves what kind of a man we would choose were we placed in the position of the doubter. Do we look for light from the man of one idea? From the man of one book, one remedy for all? What would be the good? We know the answer before we put the question to him. More probably, we search out an adviser who can be expected to approach our problem with the unprejudiced eye — in other words, the detached man.

Do we hope to get God's light from the man of affairs, the administrator with a sound practical judgment and a good head on his shoulders? If he is a man of prayer as well, we would have reason to — in other words, if his interior life has taught him discernment, if he has been purified by the action of grace and is detached.

Do we look to the scholar, the theologian, or the moralist? Yes, we would be safer to apply to one of these in preference to the man of common sense but no spirituality, to the man of high principle but no circumspection, or to the man of sympathy but no theology. But knowledge by itself will not help us either.

The person we want in our difficulties is someone whose soul has been weathered in suffering and whose suffering has taught him the love of others. We know that this person, even if he cannot solve our problems, will make them his own. And this will help.

From Hamlet, who asked for the man who was not passion's slave, down to the child who is lost in the street, all know the qualities they are after. Between the man who has been tempted and the one who has not, who would hesitate? Between the one who has failed and the other who has not, between the one who knows his weakness and where to find his strength, as against the other who knows neither, do we think twice?

This instinct of ours which guides us toward the kind of fellow human being who is likely to lead us out of our darkness is after all only a human discernment. It is useful to the soul as far as it goes, but what we need as we advance deeper into the spiritual life is not a natural but a supernatural instinct. In the darkness, we must walk by the Spirit, and so long as we are ready to go only by what the Spirit shows, we shall get to our destination in the end. We do not have to set ourselves to discerning; the light of the Holy Spirit does our discerning for us.

∞

Spiritual darkness leads to discernment

It is the darkness itself — and this is the perennial paradox of the spiritual life — that gives light. It is while enduring the nights that we come to discern. Understanding, counsel, wisdom, and the rest: they begin to flourish when this new mode of faith brings its complement to the work of Confirmation.

Contemplation does not do the work of Confirmation; it confirms it. Contemplation is not a sacrament, but it is a grace, and grace means light upon what to do next. Or if it does not tell you what to do, it tells you how to endure your inability to do anything.

The light that comes in the darkness of contemplation is not like white against black. It is more like black against black, but combining to make possible the act of acceptance here and now. It may not show the next act to be made, and it may not give the least assurance that the present act of acceptance and surrender is made in good faith, but at least it elicits an act of some kind that is certainly not one of rebellion. It is, although the soul may never know it, an act of love.

All this is part of the secret process by which the true wisdom is learned that can exercise the power of discernment as a habit. Wisdom and understanding are habits. Darkness is not a habit. It may last a long time, and accidentally become habitual to a particular soul, but it is not strictly a habit. For a quality to be a habit, it has to be designed to abide as something that is there to be constantly drawn upon.

The light of sanctifying grace is a habit. The lights that come out of the darkness increase the store of sanctifying grace, but they are not the same as sanctifying grace. Darkness ministers to the habits implanted by the Holy Spirit. It even explains them and expresses them, but is it not itself a habit such as the soul receives at Baptism.

It is in the nights of sense and spirit, although more particularly in the second of these, that the soul learns to depend absolutely upon God. And this necessity is not learned as you would learn of the dependence of work upon sleep. It is a truth that is forced upon the soul in the very action of the nights themselves, irrespective of the experience that accompanies it. It is as though your work, not your lack of sleep, taught you of the relationship between the two. Drowsiness merely confirms.

Depending absolutely upon God, where hitherto the dependence was divided between God and personal effort, the soul arrives at the possession of a directing faculty, an objective to work for, a principle that overrides every other and that provides its own sanctions, standards, and values.

On the gift of counsel, Père Henri Dominique Gardeil writes, "Our own personal life does not remain the same; we vary with the age, we change, we advance, we fall back. We have to adapt these powers of strength, justice, temperance, to a material essentially malleable, difficult to mold in the art-pattern of the saints. By ourselves we shall not know how to succeed." We *need* the Holy Spirit. We are *absolutely*, from moment to moment and from decision to decision, dependent upon God. It is the stripping of self in the darkness that gives us our claim on the gifts — even if we had not the claim that is ours in virtue of our Baptism.

The more complete the darkness, the more developed the dependence. So, if the dependence is to extend to every circumstance, whether interior trial or exterior happening, the darkness must be total.

It is not only that in no other way but that of darkness can a soul be wholly removed from self, but also that in no other way can a soul be brought into the closest possible relation with God. The two amount to the same thing, because in the order of grace, the one leads on to the other; but they are not the same thing. Would the darkness be really worth the pain of it if the result were negative only?

That the darkness is positive and unitive can be shown by the soul's attitude toward God while the darkness is reaching the consummation of its work. The prayer of a soul in this state is roughly this: "Lord, if it is You who are behind this condition of mine, I agree to whatever You have done, are doing, and may yet do. To me, it seems incredible that You are in the work, but I accept the incredible. From what I can see and feel, I would judge that Your purpose is being frustrated at every turn, that my own bitterness and rebellion are the greatest obstacle to Your freedom within my soul, and that I am hedged all around by elements that either prevent me from escaping to You or stand in the way of Your grace getting through to me. This is as I see it, but if You tell me that I am seeing wrong, I believe You."

To see one thing and believe another is to "empty oneself and become obedient."[189] To accept without evidence except the word of authority that the darkness of the understanding is the enlightenment of the soul is, in the strictest sense, to deny oneself for Christ. It denies the root claims of self.

To stand by and watch all one's ideas of perfection, of recollection, and of solitude turned inside out and given what appears to be an opposite meaning is to endure darkness. For, so long as one clings to those old ideas, one is not yet fully purified. So the darkness must go on. But when one has left those old ideas, one has left self. Now darkness has won, and the soul can be united to God.

[189] Cf. Phil. 2:7-8.

If God does not go from us, He cannot come to us. He said so on His last night on earth.[190] If we hold fast to the peace of the senses, which is the peace of the world, we shall never know fully the peace of the soul. So what *we* call "peace of soul" has to go.

If we fight for our ideals of religious service when God, the end of all religious service, is fighting for *us*, we shall prolong the darkness and at the same time not please God. If we make our demands of prayer when God, who is the whole meaning of prayer, is making His demands of us and we should be surrendering to Him, we show that self is not yet mortified.

Gradually God detaches us from our misconceptions. One by one, the fingers that keep us clinging to the edge of the cliff are pushed away. We have no support now except faith. The soul is being brought to the final handing over of self to the care of God.

But even here, having followed the process thus far, there is still lurking at the back of the mind the thought that some credit for the work must go to us: "I am surrendering, Lord; it is *my* act of faith that is giving You this pleasure."

Lord, give me more light (or darkness, whichever way I like to think of it) so that I may know that these things that I call mine are the gifts of grace, are lent to me by You. You are my surrender; You are my act of faith. In taking all, You are taking only Yours.

"That I may be found in Him not having *my* justice, which is of the law, but that which is of the faith of Christ Jesus, which is of God, justice in faith."[191]

---

[190] John 16:7.
[191] Phil. 3:9.

Chapter Twenty

Wait patiently for
union with God in Heaven

That in this state of darkness with which much of the present book is concerned, death is looked forward to with longing by the soul is seen from the references to it that we find in the psalms of desolation.

"Thou art my helper and protector, O my God, do not delay,"[192] sighs the psalmist in more than one place. "O Lord, how long? Turn to me, O Lord, and deliver my soul":[193] this is a familiar theme. The relief that the end of this life will bring to the soul in darkness is something to be legitimately sought.

When we turn to the New Testament, we find the same thing in the classic cry of the heart: "Who shall deliver me from the body of this death?"[194] This piece of self-revelation to the Romans is echoed in the passage to the Philippians where St. Paul writes about his "desire to be dissolved and to be with Christ" and how "to die is gain."[195] Death, then, is something

---

[192] Ps. 69:6 (RSV = Ps. 70:5).
[193] Ps. 6:4-5 (RSV= Ps. 6:3-4).
[194] Rom. 7:24.
[195] Phil. 1:23, 21.

to be prayed about, and those who long for it have the assurance that St. Paul was not above longing for it as well. But on conditions.

To die is gain only where both death and life are taken in terms of Christ. We may long for death only if we are prepared to live for Christ. To look forward to a particular relief is itself a relief, and to await in a state of ready acceptance the relief of death is for some souls the most appropriate relief to the darkness they are having to endure.

Perfection is not in dying, but in living. So long as a man wants to go on trying to love God while there is breath left in him, he is all right as regards his pursuit of perfection. Since his living is right, he may confidently enjoy the thought of his dying.

Again and again we find our examples in the lives of saints; those who have spoken or written of death have done so in words that show their eagerness for Heaven. Few, if any, have pointed out that the parting from the body is an evil. They have preferred to think of it as the greatest of goods.

How could they think of it as anything else? Souls that are on fire with the love of God must inevitably crave to be united with the source of that fire, with Love Himself. Loves tends to union, and the culmination of all charity is to be found in the union between the soul and God in Heaven. If to long for this union is natural to the loving soul, then to long for death, which is the means of attaining to it, is hardly less so.

When a man has made the will of God his whole happiness, he is happy enough to wait. To the man who views his whole life as so much material for the greater glory of God, there is only the practical problem of getting ready for death:

the question as to whether he can love God more by living or dying does not bother him. He leaves this, together with the time question, to God.

Time is such a very real factor to us that we cannot think of anything apart from it. We have to make an act of faith if we are to believe that mere time, as we know it and are greedy or resentful about it, does not weigh with God.

Always in this life we have to be coming to terms with time. We are so used to measuring things like friendship, service, work, and pleasure in relation to length of days that it is as hard to envisage an order of things in which there is no time as it is to imagine a planet in space where there is no air or over which there hangs no sky.

But eternity must be knowable to us to some degree and in some sense, or God would not have revealed it. The greatest help to the solving of the problem of death — whether as waiting for death or shrinking from it, but especially waiting for it — is the right approach to the problem of eternity. When life is understood as the life of God, the death of man falls into perspective.

The thought of eternity as consisting of God's whole infinite existence — for, primarily, it is the realm of His complete, absolute, and perfect being — and only then as the area in which our own everlasting life finds its place, should humble the soul into waiting upon the eternal wisdom of God.

It is only a very proud or a very stupid man who thinks more of his own need than of the power of God to meet it. He would be even more stupid if he failed to realize that the need itself existed only because it had been foreseen in the eternal mind of God.

How to Find God

Although we acknowledge the power and wisdom of God, we act as though temporal affairs depended upon the power and wisdom of man. We forget that the affairs of man are affairs at all only because they are the affairs of God. The more we come to think of God's will as manifested to us in our temporal affairs from its setting in eternity, the more ready we should be to meet its demand. Too often we think of God's will as finding its origin in the necessities of man.

Since there is no change or time with God, the contingencies of man are fixities with God. Temporal circumstances may be the occasion of the external utterance of God's will, which is eternal, but to imagine that anything temporal, either the end of the world or the end of a human life, can take place before God is ready for it — as it were, in a forgotten pocket of eternity — is folly.

A man who is flying in a plane some miles above the surface of the earth will enjoy the illusion of being outside the limitations of space. But if he acts as if he were outside the limitations of space, he comes to grief. While in this life, we have to cultivate a view of temporal affairs as seen from above while abiding by the law of our physical order.

Carry the aviation simile a stage further. Say your plane flies so high in the air that neither land nor sea nor cloud is visible. Not only would you get a new impression of space, but you would get a new impression of movement — that is to a say, you would get hardly any impression of movement, and none at all of speed. Yet while traveling in this upper air, you would know that people were moving about below, and that to them, with their concrete objects for measuring movement and distance and speed, the experience of three-dimensional existence must seem more real than it does to you. You would know that for all the greater immediacy and actuality of the lives led by the people on the ground, you in the sky were in fact more closely related to space and nearer to its secrets. You would know, moreover, that not one of those human beings down there could come to where you are now except by the power that has brought you there. If they want to come up, they must wait until the power is ready to take them.

For some reason, it is less of a strain upon the imagination to project ourselves into an area outside space than into a corresponding area outside time. But, then, we were never intended in this life to get to the end of infinity. It is only in the next life that we see how it is that it can have no end.

Ideas about eternity — whether we arrive at them through ideas about space or in any other way — can give us little enough in the way of knowledge; the essence of eternity is bound to escape our finite minds. But at least they can provide us with ideas that can help us to live out the time that precedes eternity.

Everything on earth is in a state of delay. We are *in via*. Everything is waiting for something. Inanimate creation no less than sensitive and rational creation is on its way somewhere. We human beings are forever becoming; not for an instant do we stop where we are. The universe is at the mercy of time.

But time is not a power of its own. Time is, like everything else, a creature of God. If created life depends so much upon time, we can remember that time hangs suspended in the eternity of God. Time may move independently of our wills — we cannot pull it out of its course for the sake of the past or the future — but every instant of it depends upon the will of God.

We cannot make time, but God can. We cannot kill time, but God can.

The point on which those who long too eagerly for death should meditate is this: having made time and given it to man, God means it to be used. Each must use his own slice of time until it is taken away from him. Perseverance is only the continued use of the gift of time. And perseverance, not death, is the crowning human virtue. Death is not a virtue at all; it is only a moment.

If the service of God is love, then love is waiting for the Beloved. There is no sanctity but the sanctity that is love, and love should be able to take separation in its stride. But the bitterness of its pain is known only by those lovers whose separation has been accompanied by the sense of estrangement.

The longing to be transformed in God so that a divine life is lived instead of a natural one, so that everlasting security can take the place of uncertainty, so that love may be enjoyed without the shadow of possible sin, so that the soul may go on giving worship to God without ever again feeling the pull of fallen nature: this is what the soul has to endure.

All this is what St. Augustine describes as "the purified soul sighing for the coming of its Spouse, and yearning for His most pure embrace." It is a yearning that is made bearable by grace. Indeed it is itself a grace. It is the dark night of charity.

Chapter Twenty-One
∞

Give yourself joyfully to God

The joy that concerns us here is the joy of the spirit, the joy that is nearer to peace than to pleasure, and nearer to love than to either peace or pleasure. It is therefore a joy that resides in the intellect and the will rather than in the lower faculties. It does not much delight the emotions; its satisfaction is for the soul itself.

It is not a joy in which there is no sorrow — because sorrow and joy can coexist in the same subject and at the same time. Nor is it one that is proof against deception — because souls can think they have true joy when they have false, can think they have no joy when in fact their trust in God is joy. But it is one that cannot be found by the worldling. It does not mix with its worldly counterpart.

It is not the kind of joy that the worldling particularly wants. The world wants enjoyment, wants *having*. True joy is not in having, but in giving.

To have, in this context, is to amass; to give is to engender. The joy that a soul engenders is not an enjoyment that is fabricated out of external material; it is a habit of soul that is possessed. Such a joy may be either natural or supernatural; it cannot be false.

It is joy as a supernatural quality, joy in the spirit, that will be considered in what follows.

∞

Joy calls for self-giving

In this giving which brings joy, two conditions must be observed: first, there must be a whole giving, or the joy as well as the gift will be not worth having; second, there must be a will to give for the sake of the recipient — in this case, God — and not merely for the sake of giving, or for the joy of giving, or for the fear of not having given enough.

When all is not given, there is no guarantee that joy will follow. It has to be everything: "Father, mother, wife, children, brothers, sisters, *yes and his own life also*."[196] The abundance of joy that comes with the life of Christ comes only to those who receive Him as Christ — that is, as the Christ who redeemed mankind by His Passion.

To count on the joy of Christ without being ready to suffer with Christ is to use the merits of Christ without taking the trouble to follow Him who merited them. It is only when we have given ourselves to Christ — which means giving ourselves to His kind of life, which was all the time under the shadow of the Cross — that we can start talking about the joy that we have earned. And by that time, we shall know that we have not earned anything. By that time, we shall know better than to start staking out our claim to joy.

The giving of our whole self means giving all the love that is in us — even the love that is given to us by others — to

---

[196] Luke 14:26.

God. He must have control over the activity of our hearts, over all that comes in as well as over all that goes out.

The giving of our whole self means allowing God to arrange our happiness for us, giving Him freedom of choice. To force our own type of happiness is to do away with our chance of finding true joy. When we give ourselves to God, we give ourselves to His happiness, not to our own. Once we have made Him our whole happiness, He gives us Himself in such a way that we learn to share His joy.

The giving of our whole self means giving all fear to God, especially the fear that we are serving Him badly and that we shall never serve Him better. It is true: we do serve Him badly. We are unprofitable servants.[197] We may never serve Him any better than at present. So be it. All this is handed over to Him in an act of trust in His mercy. For the rest, it must be left to Him. This is trust. Perfect trust means perfect love, and love that is perfect casts out fear.[198]

So it means that we give Him our past, our present, and our future. We give Him our time on earth to be spent as He wills and to come to an end when He wills. For some, it is harder to give God time than to give Him anything else. Or, put it another way, some find it harder to accept time at God's hands than any other cross. They are impatient and want to get on. But man must give Him the benefit of judging time.

"What is this that He saith, 'A little while'?" men are apt to cry out with the Apostles.[199] They get restless in the years of

[197] Luke 17:10.
[198] 1 John 4:18.
[199] John 16:18.

waiting. But the sorrow of such souls will be turned into joy. It is not even that, provided the sorrow is accepted, the joy will follow in due course. The words may surely be taken more literally, *convertetur* being understood to mean that sorrow becomes joyous, "is converted into" joy.[200] The bitterness of vinegar becomes sweet to the crucified; the pain of a mother's compassion is joy for her to endure.

Until we are on easy terms with time, then, we shall never know true joy. So long as we feel resentful either at being detained or at being hurried, we are not giving the disposition for true joy a chance. The poet who wrote, "At variance I am with life for wasting minutes of eternity" was not detached enough from time to know true joy. The poet who wrote, "I never yet could see the sun go down but I was angry in my heart" was too dependent on it.

This giving of our whole self that we have been considering means handing over to God the free disposing of life, of vocation, and of circumstances. It means allowing Him to produce what effects He wills, and when He wills, from the hopes we have and the efforts we make.

Failing this aspect of our gift to God, whatever joy we have will be subject to disappointment. But just as joy must be proof against fear, so it must also be proof against failure of endeavor. We shall have to rise above the sense of wasted energy, the sight of unsatisfactory returns, or our joy will get broken to bits against the rock of frustration.

We must learn accordingly to distinguish between a result and an outcome. A result is the work we try to achieve, the

---

[200] John 16:20.

required effect of labor, the mark or impression proposed. The outcome is what in fact happens. We are right to aim at results; we are wrong to be dejected by the consequences.

Results, in the sense taken here, may be conceptions of self. Consequences are conceptions of God. So long as we believe certain results to be desired by God, we must work all we can to attain them. But we must bow in submission to the outcome. It is in the outcome more than in the original impulse or in the actual prosecution of the work that the will of God can be most clearly recognized.

This is not to say that neither the inspiration of a work nor the effort expended in it matters. Obviously, they matter more than the result, as it is the point of the present argument to prove. It is to say that the appearance of failure is not to be taken as evidence of failure, and that joy must be maintained within the ruins of defeat.

We shall have to "judge not according to appearance but according to just judgment"[201] if our joy is not at the mercy of human opinion. If, while trying to serve God in full perfection, we still try to form our judgments according to ordinary ways of estimating the value of desire, of prayer, of secret and apparently wasted suffering, of cause and effect, we shall be torn between the rival joys of the world and the spirit. And we shall enjoy neither.

"Senseless man," cries St. Paul, "that which thou sowest is not quickened unless it die first."[202] Our human judgments have to die; our understanding of happiness and of success and

[201] John 7:24.
[202] 1 Cor. 15:36.

of what is meant by the perfect life of faith and love has to die; we have to rise up new creatures in Christ if we would possess the joy of Christ. Particularly is this the case if we would hand on His joy to others.

For the completeness of the gift to God, there must be the giving of prayer. This implies more than just praying; it implies giving over to God the direction and the operation of our prayer, letting Him handle it so as to allow us no say in its process and to take away from it — if He judges fit — all sense of security.

To give his prayer to God in this way is to give what touches the interior man closest. From the outset, on the day that he began the spiritual life, he has envisaged giving his power of human love to God. That he should now be called to surrender his power of loving God as well as his power of loving people is almost more than he bargained for, nor does it seem to make sense. But it is the only way to the life of pure faith.

Not until the manner of the soul's progress toward union with God has been left unqualified to the disposition of grace can the soul be said to have abandoned itself wholly to the will and love of God. The pace of advance, the changes from one state to another, the direct and indirect fruits, the direct and indirect trials: all this is at His disposal.

If it is objected that this last condition of self-giving precludes the idea of finding joy, then the answer is simply that it does. But so also does the idea of the seed dying preclude the idea of the seed living.[203] That a man must lose his life in order

---

[203] John 12:24.

to find his life[204] is a contradiction according to human wisdom, but it is a fact of experience to those who are moving in the spirit.

It is only when a man has given up all claim on joy, natural and supernatural so far as this present life is concerned, that he is ready to know what real joy is. In some cases, it is only when people have given up all hope of joy in this life, natural and supernatural, that they find themselves experiencing quite a new joy at an undiscovered level in their souls.

But nothing of this secret interior happiness can declare itself without both assiduous and unconditional prayer. The happiness is not so much *in* the prayer as *because of* the prayer. Indeed, there may be no joy in the actual exercise, but only weariness and a sense of impotence and disgust.

Lacking gladness in prayer, the soul will be glad to pray. This, because it means generosity, matters far more than devotion. Generosity again, self-giving, is the only sure test both of joy and of love.

Devotion may come and go; aridity may come and go: the soul is never kept in the same spiritual mood for long. What signifies is not the mood, but the soul's continued exercise of love in the face of variations of mood.

"I have learned in whatsoever state I am," St. Paul admits to the Philippians, "to be content therewith. I know how to be brought low, and I know how to abound. Everywhere and in all things, I am instructed."[205] Here is detachment. Here is the fruit of self-giving. Here is, in effect, joy.

[204] Matt. 10:39.
[205] Phil. 4:11-12.

"I can do all things in Him who strengthens me,"[206] St. Paul goes on. All things — I can even rejoice.

∞

Joy calls for generous giving

The second condition in the activity of giving — namely, that it should be for the benefit of the recipient and not for the pleasure of it — is no less important than the first. Failure to fulfill the second condition proves that the first has not been fulfilled either. If I make my sacrifice in the hope of finding joy at last, I am not giving up myself, but rather taking myself with me. I am establishing myself as the recipient of my own gift — a ridiculous position to occupy.

There are many good people who give for the sake of giving, and it is to be hoped that they will gain supernatural merit. There are three quite separate factors at work in the act of giving — natural generosity, vainglory, and supernatural generosity — and although they tend to intermingle, the quality that is uppermost in the will determines the character of the act.

It is the element of vainglory in the act of giving that reduces the chances of joy. Natural generosity brings its own joys; they are real and worthwhile, but unrelated, except indirectly, to the life of prayer, which is the main concern of this book. Supernatural generosity, as we have seen above, brings its own joys; they are far more worthwhile than the others, but nobody who has not experienced them will be able to see how they can feel at all real.

[206] Phil. 4:13.

Within the sweep of vainglory would be included more than merely the hope of winning recognition. Vainglory is any sort of satisfaction to self that is looked for in preference to the glory of God. I can glorify myself vainly by stirring up artificial devotion in prayer, by taking up penance as an escape, or by doing works of charity for the glow of well-being that accompanies them.

Lastly, it is the fear of not giving that prejudices the perfection of the gift. The whole thing becomes now too reflexive: the giver is more occupied with himself and his dreads than with Him to whom he is supposed to be surrendering himself in an act of love.

"Are my motives good enough? Am I doing this because I am afraid? Do I really love God? Is the gift worthwhile? I shall never be happy if I do not give — and give more and give now. Never happy? Well, in that case, I must. But it will not please God when I give like this, simply because I am afraid of offending Him if I do not — or worse, because I am afraid of being unhappy."

And so it goes on. Meanwhile, the gold tarnishes, and what love there once was in all this wears thin. There is no joy in all this.

Better not to look at the gift, but look at the Person you are giving it to. Better not to look at yourself, at your crisscross of different selves, at your doubts and your fears and your desires for joy. It only confuses the main thing, which is love. Nothing else matters. Leave joy aside; that can follow after. It is a by-product anyhow.

"I do not count myself to have apprehended. But one thing I do: forgetting the things that are behind, and stretching forth myself to those that are before, I press toward the mark, to the prize of the supernal vocation of God in Christ Jesus."[207]

Once the soul has learned to love and pray and think objectively, the question of joy solves itself. It comes at the disposal of grace. The interior life is not the introspective life. Mystics are not automagnetic. If the life of prayer teaches a man anything, it is that God is responsible for his life and prayer and thought, and that the more he goes out of himself into God, the better. It is the man of prayer who sees more clearly than other men that Christ is indeed the life of the soul, the light of the world. Everything else is borrowed. God alone is life itself and light itself.

God is joy, too; joy is inseparable from life and from love. Christ has come that we might have life and joy, and have them more abundantly.[208] He has come also that we might have love, and that is why we have suffering as well as joy. Suffering, not joy, is the appropriate act of love.

"Greater love than this no man hath: that he should lay down his life."[209] But in laying down his life with Christ, the follower of Christ finds joy. Although he may not know it, it is because he has already found love. It is what he has been searching for all along.

"For when I seek Thee, my God, I seek the blessed life. I will seek Thee that my soul may live. For my body lives by my soul, and my soul lives by Thee."[210]

---

[207] Phil. 3:13-14.

[208] Cf. John 10:10.

[209] John 15:13.

[210] St. Augustine, *Confessions*, Bk. 10, ch. 20.

Chapter Twenty-Two

Follow Christ, the Way

The whole of man's conflict is because he is forever searching for truth and forever stopping short at half-truth. Yet search he must, even though he knows that with this half-truth in his hand, he will search with a divided mind. His hope is always that he will discover enough of truth to keep his mind quiet, and that then he can forget about the truth that has yet to be known. In this hope, he is constantly disappointed, for everything that he learns about truth points to something more to be learned.

So the mind of man goes on searching and refusing to search, saying it has had enough and always wanting more, ever on the alert to see and then too afraid to look, living restlessly and dissatisfied on what it has found and, at the same time, rejecting the good to which his partial discovery has given him the entry.

He may imagine that he is getting nearer to truth by splitting it into bits — scientific truth, psychological truth, philosophical truth, metaphysical truth — and trying to live in one of them. As if truth were a row of villas you could choose from. As if truth could be divided. As if natural truth bore no relation to supernatural truth.

Life and truth hang together. Man really only lives in the measure that he apprehends truth. Yet because he will not look in the right direction for truth, or dare not face it where he suspects it to be, he is condemned to a life that is not a life. Without Christ, who is Truth, life is empty.

"You will not come to me that you may have life,"[211] says our Lord in the fifth chapter of St. John. But our one chance is to come to Him. He does not point the way; He *is* the way. We want truth and life; He *is* the truth and the life.[212]

We crave life everlasting as we crave truth everlasting, but "he who heareth my word and believeth Him who sent me hath life everlasting."[213] Why do men talk so much about fumbling their way toward truth and stumbling over faith? "God has given us understanding" says St. John in his first letter, "that we may know the true God and be in His true Son. This is the true God and eternal life."[214] Truth and life: both in Christ.

There is the same invitation to wisdom, knowledge, truth and life in the Old Testament. "All you who thirst, come to the waters," cries Isaiah. "Incline your ear and come; hear and your soul shall live."[215] The appeal rings through the prophetic writings like the Temple bell. But the trouble with the world is always the same: it cannot face obeying God, and cannot quite deny Him.

[211] John 5:40.
[212] John 14:6.
[213] John 5:24.
[214] 1 John 5:20.
[215] Isa. 55:1, 3.

In the man of the world, we can understand this infirmity of purpose — he is distracted; he is lured away; he never sees the issue in its sharpest outline — but should we condone it in the man of God? The man of God, if anyone, should be able to say with St. Paul that he counts all things to be but loss for the excellent knowledge of Jesus Christ his Lord.[216] His whole purpose is to know Christ, and Him crucified.[217] If he fails in this, there is no value to him; he is no man of God.

"That I may know Him, and the power of His resurrection and the fellowship of His sufferings, being made conformable to His death."[218] Such is the purpose of the man of God: knowledge, suffering, and conformity. So long as he wants to know, and wants to follow up what his knowledge tells him, the man of God will be a true man of God; he will be a lover of God.

According to Pascal,[219] there are only two kinds of sensible people: those who serve God with all their hearts because they know Him, and those who seek Him with all their hearts because they do not."

"Truth," says St. Thomas, "must be the last end of the whole universe, and the consideration of truth must be the chief occupation of wisdom." This is to ask a good deal of a universe wrapped in materialism, but it should not be too much to ask of a wisdom schooled in contemplation. Anyway

---

[216] Phil. 3:8.

[217] 1 Cor. 2:2.

[218] Phil. 3:10.

[219] Blaise Pascal (1623-1662), French theologian, mathematician, and savant.

it is what God asks. And He has made the universe and is responsible for wisdom.

St. Thomas further points out that Divine Wisdom, clothed in the flesh, declares that He came into the world to make known the truth.[220]

Before the coming of Christ, and among the Gentiles to whom revelation meant no more than a sectarian literature, it was recognized that man was in labor to bring forth knowledge. Even now, after the Word has revealed His wisdom, man is still a pilgrim and a stranger. He knows what he is looking for, and where to find it, but he walks by faith in an alien land. He lacks the knowledge that his soul craves.

Aristotle[221] defines the first philosophy as being "the knowledge of truth . . . not the knowledge of any truth, but of that truth which is the source of all truth; of that, namely, which refers to the first principle of being."

We Christians know what the first principle of being is: it is love. We do not have to break our heads against the problem of what aspect of truth it is that is the source of all truth. We know that God is charity and that God is the source of all. Truth and love are inseparable.

In our own experience, is not our search for truth the same as our search for love? Do we not know that whatever we find of one we find of the other? To some souls, it may well seem that the intellect is more engaged than the will; to others, that the will is more engaged than the intellect. But either way you look at it, it is the one soul stretching out to the one good.

---

[220] John 18:37.

[221] Aristotle (384-322 B.C.), Greek philosopher.

Sometimes we feel that we have at last laid hold of reality, and that things will never be insecure again. Or we feel that we have found in charity at last the two-edged sword that in the same act separates our love of God from self and our love of others from inordinate affection. While in this state, we wonder what it could have been that had kept us for so long from seeing and loving; we feel we should have known how to do it all along. "It is clear now; I understand. Love and truth are one, and all I have to do is go on as I am. I do not have to be afraid of loving anymore. It is not selfish after all."

And then our faces get smacked down on the pavement again, and we are back where we were before. But this is all right; it is quite in order. We are not suffered to see things clearly for long; we may not always love without the haunting fears that accompany our love and keep it safe. If all were to run so smoothly, where would be the faith? And would we not soon become complacent, indifferent, and rash? No, better and safer to conduct our search at ground level. But the question is an academic one, since it is not in our power to choose.

∞

Following Christ ultimately brings peace

If Christ "came into this world to make known the truth," then those who follow Christ and share His life must have the same work at heart. *Bonitas est diffusiva sui,*[222] and since truth and love are goodness itself they must spread. The followers of Christ are those who are chosen to help in the spread of truth and love.

---

[222] "His goodness is diffusive."

As to how any given soul will further Christ's work of communicating this knowledge to the world must depend upon the nature of his particular vocation. If the responsibility rests upon one soul more than upon another, it is upon the soul that sees more and loves more.

Just as there are two kinds of searchers for truth and love — the kind who do their seeking and loving among their fellowmen, and those who leave the world and try to work out their problems by the light of grace in solitude — so there are two kinds of apostles. One kind goes about in the world teaching truth and penetrating with love "the million masks of God." The other kind fights the untruth within his own soul and, from his solitude, works for the love of man.

Whether he serves truth and charity among men or on his own, the man who sets out for the full apostolate of love will sooner or later come to see more of life and of reality than if he had set out for nothing but personal experience. His search in the blindness of faith will reveal to him what he could never have learned by wide-eyed study.

The man who struggles among men for the love of God may come to see as much of his vileness as the other who struggles in secret, but at least he will have other things to occupy his mind. The man who is alone will see his own vileness and will have God as his sole refuge.

The man who works in the world may come to feel as much estranged from God and from his fellowmen as the other who works in the monastery, but at least he will know that he is laboring for souls. The man who is alone will come to doubt if he labors for anyone but himself. And he will feel that even this has been proved useless.

But all this is incalculably worthwhile. Incalculable in the strict sense: "Neither has it entered into the heart of man what things God has prepared for them who love Him."[223] Throughout the night, the soul must keep it as a fact close to the heart that the joy that will declare itself eventually is out of all proportion to the present pain, and that in the light of the dawn, one will be glad of having gone through the darkness. Although the soul must cling to this belief, it is doubtful that it will bring much comfort at the time.

The very inability to find what one is looking for is itself a sign that interiorly the discovery has already been made. It proves that one is still looking, and it is this that guarantees the ultimate revelation. In this life, it *is* the revelation.

So long as the soul is drawn across the desert by the power of some vestige of hope — believing that in spite of the disappointments and failures, there must be an answer and a satisfaction — there is evidence that at a level that brings no assurance now, the beginnings of victory are already achieved. What the soul cannot see, because it is not meant to see, is that the search is as much God's as one's own. It is because God is searching for us that we are moved to search for Him.

In this continuous quest of ours on earth, we should realize that we are exiles rather than explorers — that we belong to Him and therefore must be always looking for Him. We tend to think of it too much the other way around: that He belongs to us and that therefore we cannot be happy without Him.

Where there are two ways of looking at spiritual truths, the way that brings us closer to reality is the one that looks at the

---

[223] 1 Cor. 2:9.

truth from God's angle rather than from our own. Always our prayer remains that of the blind man at Jericho's gate: "Lord, that I may see."[224]

But let me see in Your terms, not my own. If I see as I want to see, I shall see only what I want to see, and, in that case, it is better not to see at all. I must see life as You see it. I must see people, suffering, love, joy, peace, and sin through Your eyes if I am to use them for Your glory. If I view my life with the eyes of sense, I may learn something about my surroundings but I shall learn little about myself and about You.

How can I make true deductions from facts that I see only partially? If significant facts are understood superficially, they cannot be said to signify. For instance, if I take results to be the true measure of effort, I am making a false inference and generalization from a fact that may well be true in a particular case, but that is not essentially understood. I am missing the point about three things: about effort, about results, and about the relationship between the two.

To judge in this way is no less to judge according to the senses than to conclude from a person's face that he is not to be trusted. If I am looking for truth, I must refuse to be dictated to by the senses. Once the outward means more to me as a standard of valuation, as a guide to conduct, as a qualification of merit, than the inward, I am virtually eliminating the principle of motive. Certainly I am discounting the work of grace.

In proportion as outward results are trusted in as offering the surest indications available, the life of faith diminishes. How can environment and circumstances be seen as planned

---

[224] Mark 10:51.

by Providence when the created order is seen as a combination of necessary effects following given causes?

To judge according to the spirit and not according to the flesh requires faith, and faith cannot come to the perfection of its exercise unless it has been subjected to the pressure of the senses and has overcome. In the night of the senses, the soul is weaned from the influence of sense persuasions; in the night of the spirit, the soul learns to judge in the spirit.

In the night of the senses, the soul is purified as regards knowledge that is untrue; in the night of the spirit, the soul acquires knowledge that is true.

In the night of the senses, the soul is forced to shed its natural mode of learning and praying and loving; in the night of the spirit, the soul is given a new mode of learning and praying and loving.

In the night of the senses, it is the lower faculties of the soul that feel the darkness most; in the night of the spirit, it is the intellect and will that suffer mostly.

Whether in the night of sense or of spirit, whether affected in the lower or higher faculties, the soul suffers because it searches. The soul that is not serious in searching enters neither the night of sense nor the night of spirit. But just because it is our search that makes us suffer, it is our suffering that brings us finally to the object of our search. A suffering that has nothing in it of the search for God is a wasted suffering. A search for God that has nothing in it of suffering is, in our Christian dispensation, an anomaly.

If we search in Christ, who is also the object of our search, we search in the wounds of Christ and in the desolation of Christ. But we search also in the peace of Christ, the peace that the world cannot give.[225] It is a curious sort of peace that our searching brings, and by the world it would not be called peace at all; it is the peace that you feel when you know you cannot do anything else but what you are doing, and that there is nothing worse to be afraid of.

It is a peace that may not bring great joy to the heart, or even tranquillity to the nerves, but somewhere deep in the soul there is the obscure knowledge that you will find yourself at rest eventually in God. Whatever life is like now, the time must come when your essential being will be caught up into your true vocation, which is love. And this is peace.

∞

Love, truth, and peace are found in Christ

All men must search. Just as in the physical order, all are drawn by gravitational attraction to the center of the universe, so in the spiritual order, all are drawn to the center of being, which is God. Some respond to the attraction; others do not. But whether they admit it or refuse it, the attraction is there. And it keeps men reaching for it.

No civilization has yet been produced that has forsworn the pursuit of truth. Until the end of the world, men's minds will go on feeling toward truth, and to the extent that they are directed toward the Source of truth, men will possess life and freedom. It is strange that after the philosophers and theologians and preachers have had their say, so much remains still to be explained, so much remains still to be sought. But it is not strange really, if we recognize the function of faith. That is

---

[225] Cf. John 14:27.

why the mystics can tell us more than the philosophers. That is why God reveals Himself to the weak, the fools, and the children[226] — because they have to possess faith if they are to get along at all. And possessing faith, they learn by love and experience what others have to pick up with study.

But for mystic and philosopher, the principle of true wisdom is the same. It comes from one origin and moves to one end. Its common doctrine is that apart from God, there is no solution — there are only escapes.

We look for a formula, and our formula is the Word. We look for love, and Christ is Love: You alone are holy; You alone are the Lord; You alone are the Most High, Jesus Christ.

We look for peace, and again we find it in Him: "In You, Lord, I have hoped; may I never be put to shame."[227] He is our hope; He is our life. Christ is All.

[226] Matt. 11:25; Luke 10:21.
[227] Cf. Ps. 30:2 (RSV = Ps. 31:1).

Biographical note
∞

Dom Hubert van Zeller
(1905-1984)

Dom Hubert van Zeller was born in 1905 of English parents in Alexandria, Egypt, where his father was in military service during the time when the country was a British protectorate. Van Zeller was educated privately until the age of nine, when he was sent for the remainder of his schooling to the Benedictine Abbey at Downside, England. Upon completing his education at the age of eighteen, he spent a year working at a Liverpool cotton firm before entering the novitiate at Downside in 1924. Unsettled and distracted by his school duties and desiring a more austere way of life, he struggled with his vocation at Downside for many years, even leaving for a brief period in the 1930s to enter the stricter Carthusian monastery at Parkminster.

After his return to Downside, van Zeller became more involved in giving retreats and in writing on spiritual matters. By the time of his death in 1984, he had written scores of books on prayer and spirituality, which won him a devoted readership throughout the English-speaking world. In addition to being a writer, van Zeller was a prolific and talented sculptor, whose works grace many churches and monasteries in Britain and the United States.

How to Find God

Although a friend of Oxford-educated Catholic writers such as Ronald Knox and Evelyn Waugh, van Zeller once described his own writing about the Faith as an effort to use "the idiom of every day to urge people of every day to embark upon the spirituality of every day." Written with moving depth and simplicity, van Zeller's books should be read by all Christians seeking to pray and serve with greater fidelity in these difficult days.

An Invitation

Reader, the book that you hold in your hands was published by Sophia Institute Press. Sophia Institute seeks to nurture the spiritual, moral, and cultural life of souls and to spread the Gospel of Christ in conformity with the authentic teachings of the Roman Catholic Church.

Our press fulfills this mission by offering translations, reprints, and new publications that afford readers a rich source of the enduring wisdom of mankind.

We also operate two popular online Catholic resources: CrisisMagazine.com and CatholicExchange.com.

Crisis Magazine provides insightful cultural analysis that arms readers with the arguments necessary for navigating the ideological and theological minefields of the day. *Catholic Exchange* provides world news from a Catholic perspective as well as daily devotionals and articles that will help you to grow in holiness and live a life consistent with the teachings of the Church.

Sophia Institute Press also serves as the publisher for the Thomas More College of Liberal Arts and Holy Spirit College. Both colleges provide university-level education under the guiding light of Catholic teaching. If you know a young person seeking a college that takes seriously the adventure of learning and the quest for truth, please bring these institutions to his attention.

www.SophiaInstitute.com
www.CatholicExchange.com
www.CrisisMagazine.com